Ronald Reagan and the Firing of the Air Traffic Controllers

LANDMARK PRESIDENTIAL DECISIONS

Series Editor
Michael Nelson

Advisory Board
Meena Bose
Brendan J. Doherty
Richard J. Ellis
Lori Cox Han
James Oakes
Barbara A. Perry
Andrew Rudalevige

Ronald Reagan and the Firing of the Air Traffic Controllers

Andrew E. Busch

University Press of Kansas

© 2024 by the University Press of Kansas
All rights reserved

Published by the University Press of Kansas (Lawrence, Kansas 66045), which was organized by the Kansas Board of Regents and is operated and funded by Emporia State University, Fort Hays State University, Kansas State University, Pittsburg State University, the University of Kansas, and Wichita State University.

Library of Congress Cataloging-in-Publication Data

Names: Busch, Andrew, author.
Title: Ronald Reagan and the firing of the air traffic controllers / Andrew E. Busch.
Description: Lawrence, Kansas : University Press of Kansas, 2024. | Series: Landmark presidential decisions | Includes bibliographical references and index.
Identifiers: LCCN 2023049656 (print) | LCCN 2023049657 (ebook)
  ISBN 9780700636907 (cloth)
  ISBN 9780700636914 (paperback)
  ISBN 9780700636921 (ebook)
Subjects: LCSH: Air Traffic Controllers' Strike, U.S., 1981. | Professional Air Traffic Controllers Organization (Washington, D.C.) | Reagan, Ronald. | Collective labor agreements—Air traffic controllers—United States.
Classification: LCC HD5325.A4252 1981 B87 2024 (print) | LCC HD5325.A4252 1981 (ebook) | DDC 331.892/81387740426097309048—dc23/eng/20231117
LC record available at https://lccn.loc.gov/2023049656.
LC ebook record available at https://lccn.loc.gov/2023049657.

British Library Cataloguing-in-Publication Data is available.

Dedicated to my students over thirty years of teaching, who have my everlasting affection and best wishes.

CONTENTS

Acronyms and Initialisms   ix

Foreword by Lori Cox Han   xi

Acknowledgments   xiii

Introduction   1

Chapter 1. The Setting   4

Chapter 2. The Cast of Characters   25

Chapter 3. Presidential Decision   39

Chapter 4. Political Reaction   65

Chapter 5. Consequences   88

Conclusion   112

Appendix A. Timeline: Ronald Reagan and the PATCO Strike   119

Appendix B. Ronald Reagan Letter to Robert E. Poli, President of the Professional Air Traffic Controllers Organization, October 20, 1981   123

Appendix C. Transcript of Reagan Remarks and Question-and-Answer Session with Reporters on the Air Traffic Controllers Strike, August 3, 1981   124

Notes   131

Bibliographic Essay   153

Index   157

ACRONYMS AND INITIALISMS

PATCO: Professional Air Traffic Controllers Organization
AFL-CIO: American Federation of Labor - Congress of Industrial Organizations
FAA: Federal Aviation Agency/Administration
ATCA: Air Traffic Control Association
MEBA: Maritime Engineers Beneficial Association
OMB: Office of Management and Budget
OPM: Office of Personnel Management
ALPA: Air Line Pilots Association
ATA: Airline Transportation Association
FLRA: Federal Labor Relations Authority
ERTA: Economic Recovery Tax Act
USATCO: United States Air Traffic Controllers Organization
NATCA: National Air Traffic Controllers Association

FOREWORD

Ronald Reagan, considered by supporters and critics alike to be a transformational political figure, left a lasting mark on presidential politics as well as the modern conservative movement. Reagan's legacy is a combination of policy successes and failures dictated by the political circumstances in which he attempted to govern, as well as his own strengths and weaknesses as a leader. In many ways, his 1981 inaugural address set an important tone for his presidency when he declared that "government is not the solution to our problems; government is the problem." Reagan's first term policy agenda focused on cutting taxes, cutting domestic policy spending, and increasing defense spending (often referred to as Reaganomics), along with a conservative social agenda (such as support for school prayer and opposition to reproductive rights) and a tougher approach to US-Soviet relations. While only one of many examples during his presidency, Reagan's firing of more than 11,000 striking air traffic controllers in August 1981 solidified his credentials with his conservative supporters.

Beyond policy, Reagan also set a new standard for his use of the symbolic powers of the presidency during his eight years in office. Television was a perfect fit for Reagan's public skills as he stepped into the role of the chief executive. The Reagan administration enjoyed unqualified success in its management of news generated by the White House as well as the image portrayed of the man in charge. Reagan became known as the "great communicator" for dominating the media environment during the 1980s. He also earned the nickname "Teflon president" during his second term since serious charges stemming from the Iran-Contra scandal never seemed to "stick" to the president. His skillful use of rhetoric was often simple, direct, and self-deprecating, which endeared Reagan to his supporters and opponents alike. His mastery of the public aspects of the office remains one of the greatest achievements of Reagan's presidency. Reagan's brand of public leadership changed an important part of presidential leadership, not only in how the White House manages the public aspects of the office but the public expectations as well. The country expects the president to regularly perform on the public stage as part of presidential events that are well scripted and produced. Reagan mastered the role of president in a changing media environment where image could, at times, matter more than substance.

As an example, Reagan's firing of the striking air traffic controllers offers a fascinating case study from the dual perspectives of public policy and public performance, explaining both the myth and the reality of the Reagan presidency. Reagan was well known for relishing symbolic victories, and his response to the strike showcased his belief in the power of individuals over that of institutions. He also skillfully flipped the narrative away from public sympathy for the striking workers to support for his actions as president. While the strike was a significant event in 1981, with the obvious implications for air travel and its connection to the American economy if the strike continued, the story itself did not rise to the level of something along the lines of an international and/or military crisis. However, Reagan leveraged the situation into an opportunity to showcase his convictions on the matter through a dramatic public confrontation. As Andrew Busch describes in this analysis of the PATCO strike, Reagan gained political prestige through his actions that backed up his tough rhetoric on the issue, and as a result, public opinion favored him over the striking air traffic controllers. Part of the eventual Reagan legacy came to life with his words and deeds on this particular issue, showcasing the emphasis on style, image, and symbolism so prevalent during the Reagan administration.

When he left office in 1989, Reagan had made an indelible mark on not only the Republican Party and the modern conservative movement, but also on how presidents can use, and sometimes manipulate, the rhetorical powers available to the office. Reagan's personal style and skill as a communicator, coupled with his pragmatic approach to politics, often belied the strong ideological shift to the right that occurred during Reagan's presidency. While many Americans often disagreed with his policy positions, they tended to like Reagan as a person. As such, he is remembered as a once-in-a-generation leader within the Republican Party and has cast a long shadow over the presidents, both Republican and Democrat, who have followed.

Lori Cox Han
Chapman University

ACKNOWLEDGMENTS

As is noted throughout the book, I am thoroughly indebted to the accounts of these events published by scholars, journalists, and participants. I am also grateful for the assistance rendered by the staff of the Reagan Library and by my excellent student research assistant, Mr. Cary Dornier, as well as the support of the Rose Institute of State and Local Government at Claremont McKenna College.

Introduction

The Professional Air Traffic Controllers Organization strike that began on August 3, 1981, has been the subject of substantial scholarly attention over the last four decades. However, for the most part, that work has been done by labor historians and economists interested in studying the issue with a focus on PATCO and the labor movement more generally. The PATCO strike as the occasion of a significant presidential decision, with a focus on President Ronald Reagan, his administration, and the political response and consequences, deserves much more attention than it has received.

Reagan's momentous decision was to fire the strikers, ban them from federal employment, prosecute strike leaders, and seek to decertify the union. That decision (or complex of decisions) was risky, but it worked for Reagan, both substantively and politically. It was bracketed by two other noteworthy decisions: before the strike, to offer PATCO a pay raise that would have broken through previous conventions of negotiation with a federal employee union, and after the firings, to steadfastly refuse to rehire the strikers despite considerable pressure to do so. The import of the negotiating strategy was negated when PATCO struck anyway; the refusal to rehire the strikers, while crucial, was derivative of the firing itself. But they were all part of the story. Reagan's last two decisions had a number of crucial consequences, only some (and not necessarily the clearest) of which had to do with the future of organized labor in the United States.

This book will explore exactly those questions—the PATCO crisis as a case study of a key presidential decision.

Chapter 1 examines the setting, starting with Reagan's background, his rise to the presidency, the challenges facing his administration, and the successes of his first six months in office. It moves on to a detailed look at the rise of PATCO after its formation in 1968 and how the union came to the edge of a nationwide strike.

Chapter 2 sketches the Reagan administration figures who played important roles in the crisis, as well as Reagan's approach to managing his administration. Key PATCO figures and outsiders ranging from congressmen to leaders of other unions are also included.

Chapter 3 gets to the heart of the matter. How did PATCO and the Reagan administration reach an impasse that led to the strike? How did Reagan and his people negotiate with the union and then, failing that, reach and implement the decision to fire the strikers, decertify the union, and prosecute strike leaders? And how did Reagan deal with subsequent pressure to rehire them? In retrospect, it is clear that Reagan wanted to accommodate PATCO as far as he thought prudence would permit, but had long before determined that he would take a firm stand if the union crossed the line into an illegal strike.

Chapter 4 explores the response of the broader political system to Reagan's policy decision. Public opinion writ large, the coordinate branches of Congress and the courts, the media, and a variety of interest groups—especially other unions—are the subjects of consideration. On balance, the political system harbored little support for the strikers. Reagan's decision to fire them was popular, and those who might have assisted the strike were, at best, ambivalent and disarmed. The public was more divided about whether to rehire the strikers after the dust had settled.

Chapter 5 turns to both the short- and long-term consequences of Reagan's decision. In the short term, effects on the economy, air travel, and the union itself are reviewed. Long-term consequences include the impact on labor-management relations in the United States, effects on the fight against inflation and on political/electoral coalitions, impact on the presidency, and international consequences. Some of these effects are at times exaggerated by analysts—Reagan did not single-handedly destroy the American labor movement, which had been on a downward trajectory for nearly three decades already, by firing the PATCO strikers. But taken together, the consequences were quite significant, even in foreign policy, where one might have expected them to be negligible.

Finally, a brief conclusion works to bring these elements together in a cohesive way and asks questions including: What does the PATCO crisis reveal about Reagan's leadership and administrative management? What broader lessons can be learned from this presidential decision?

The plane is at the gate. It originated in Philadelphia, in a paper written for the 2006 American Political Science Conference, though it rested undisturbed in the maintenance hangar for many years after that. When Michael Nelson and the University Press of Kansas offered an opportunity (and deadline) for the plane to be refurbished and upgraded, the author gratefully accepted and got to work. It is time to board. Enjoy the flight.

CHAPTER 1

The Setting

On August 3, 1981, the president was facing a crisis of significant scope. The president was Ronald Reagan, fortieth president of the United States. The crisis was a conflict with the Professional Air Traffic Controllers Organization, or PATCO.

Air traffic controllers were federal employees indispensable to the nation's system of air transport, responsible for tracking and guiding both commercial and private air traffic from departure to landing. They were, consequently, responsible for the safety of tens of thousands of airline passengers daily although, unlike the pilots who flew the planes, they were almost entirely invisible to the public, squirreled away in airport control towers or in regional air traffic control facilities.

The controllers had formed PATCO in 1968, and by 1981 the organization claimed about fourteen thousand members among the nation's seventeen thousand air traffic controllers. Although the word "union" was not part of its name, it functioned as one, pushing for higher pay, shorter hours, and increased benefits. As federal employees, the controllers were barred by law from going on strike. In addition, they took an oath upon employment promising not to strike, and a federal judge had issued a permanent injunction against PATCO strikes in 1970. Nevertheless, it was, in the judgment of both outside observers and Reagan administration analysts, one of the most aggressive of the public employee unions. PATCO had taken at least six "job actions" between 1968 and 1981 and had consequently gained concessions from each of the three administrations prior to Reagan's, though in a few instances a handful of controllers faced disciplinary action.[1] Air traffic controllers had one of the highest paying public sector jobs in America, although they also had persistent concerns about job stress, especially at the nation's busiest airports and control centers, aging equipment, and consistently poor relations with the Federal Aviation Administration under which they operated.[2]

The organization's new leadership, including president Robert E. Poli, observed that controllers and other federal employees had engaged in job actions in the past without consequence despite the law, and they calculated that the controllers were so essential to air traffic, and air traffic so essential to the national economy, that they could not be fired. As one of the few unions to endorse Ronald Reagan in 1980, they also counted on a friendly White House. Their job was so important and stressful, Poli and his lieutenants reasoned, that they deserved more—much more—and that the government would ultimately deliver.[3] Poli and the union rolled the dice on a big ask undergirded by a big threat: We will walk off the job if need be. On August 3, the walkout began.

The View from the White House

Although negotiations directly involved the Federal Aviation Administration and the Department of Transportation, the ultimate decisions about how to handle PATCO's demands and the strike were in Reagan's hands. So what was the view from the White House?

First, one must take into account Reagan's personal biography. He had come of age politically during the New Deal and had voted for Franklin Roosevelt four times. As an actor in Hollywood, he rose in the ranks of the Screen Actors Guild—the union for film actors—first joining the guild's board of directors as a representative of the younger actors. In 1946, he played a role in stopping an attempt by the Communist-affiliated Conference of Studio Unions to displace an independent union as the representative of set erectors. Through the late 1940s, he was said by Sterling Hayden to be "a one-man battalion of opposition" to the Communist infiltration of Hollywood.[4] In 1947, Reagan became president of the Screen Actors Guild, his first term of five. In 1960, in his final term as SAG president, he led the union's first ever strike against the studios.

By that time, Reagan had undergone a significant political transformation. In the 1950s, he found himself supporting Dwight D. Eisenhower's Republican presidential runs and becoming an avid reader of the newly-founded conservative journal *National Review.* As his movie career waned, he became a national spokesman for General Electric, travelling the country and extolling the benefits of free enterprise. Realizing that he had not voted for a Democratic presidential candidate since Harry S. Truman in 1948, Reagan formally switched parties, declaring himself a Republican in 1962.[5] In 1964, he was launched onto the national political stage when he delivered a fundraising speech for Barry Goldwater which was successful enough that the Goldwater campaign replayed it on national television.

Goldwater lost badly, and Reagan became the new spokesman for the conservative cause. His stance paralleled the so-called fusionism of the *National Review:* strong anti-communism, support for limited government and free enterprise, and a social or moral traditionalism. After being encouraged to run by a group of California businessmen who had been inspired by "The Speech," Reagan was elected governor of California in 1966, defeating the venerable two-term incumbent governor Pat Brown by over a million votes. He was then reelected handily in 1970. As both supporters and opponents had expected, Reagan forged a generally conservative record as governor, but he was relatively moderate in his policies toward labor, signing a bill allowing local governments to engage in collective bargaining and earning him the distrust of the state's right-to-work committee. Nevertheless, he admired Calvin Coolidge, who was catapulted to the Republican vice-presidential nomination in 1920 because of his firm hand in breaking a police strike in Boston while governor of Massachusetts. During that episode, Coolidge famously said that "There is no right to strike against the public safety by anybody, anywhere, at any time"—a mantra that Reagan would later turn against PATCO. As governor of California, Reagan faced two major public employee strikes with firmness but flexibility. In one case, he mobilized replacements for striking Sacramento firefighters, calling on State Division of Forestry firefighters to fill in; the Sacramento firemen returned to work. In another case, when State Water Resources Department employees struck, Reagan threatened to fire them, as state law mandated, if they did not return within five days. On the fifth day they returned. Negotiations continued during the walkouts, and both strikes resulted in raises.[6]

Between his governorship and his presidency, Reagan had a syndicated radio commentary on issues of current concern which played on nearly three hundred radio stations. On May 25, 1977, Reagan delivered a broadcast entitled "Public Servants," in which he laid out his views on public employee strikes. In retrospect, the broadcast anticipated exactly what Reagan's response would be to PATCO's walkout. He began the commentary by quoting Franklin Roosevelt's disdain of public employee strikes. He then amplified it, holding that a strike by public employees is a strike against the people, their ultimate employers. Highlighting the threat posed by such strikes, Reagan noted that in a recent fiscal year, 316,000 government workers at all levels engaged in a total of 490 "unauthorized & illegal work stoppages." With this as a backdrop, Reagan concluded by endorsing an attempt by some California teachers to amend the state constitution to ban public employee strikes. Violations would result in "mandatory dismissal," and "Anyone dismissed for striking could not be reinstated."[7]

Meanwhile, throughout the 1970s, as Keynesianism encountered stagflation, as détente seemed to embolden Soviet aggression, and as numerous key social indices floundered, conservatism gained strength. Reagan narrowly failed to win the Republican presidential nomination against incumbent Gerald Ford in 1976, but came back in 1980 to get the Republican nod. In the general election, Reagan convincingly defeated incumbent president Jimmy Carter, winning forty-four states and 489 electoral votes to Carter's six states, DC, and forty-nine electoral votes. In the nationally aggregated popular vote, Reagan won 51 percent to Carter's 41 percent and independent John Anderson's 7 percent. Reagan won traditional Republican strongholds in the Midwest. He also won the South, much of which his campaign thought was Carter's until late in the game, and even Massachusetts, the only state won by George McGovern in Richard Nixon's 1972 presidential sweep.[8]

Making his victory even more striking, Reagan was joined by the first Republican Senate since 1954 when the GOP gained twelve seats in the chamber, defeating such liberal Democratic stalwarts as George McGovern, Frank Church, John Culver, and Warren Magnuson. In the House of Representatives, Republicans gained thirty-three seats, not enough for a party majority but enough to forge a cross-party majority with conservative Democrats.

During the campaign, Reagan's relationship with America's unions was strained. On the campaign trail, he frequently touted his record as president of the Screen Actors Guild, but the AFL-CIO and most other unions endorsed Jimmy Carter. (Democratic Senator Ted Kennedy was the favorite of many unionists but had failed in his primary challenge to Carter.) Overall, only four unions endorsed Reagan—the Teamsters, the Maritime Engineers Beneficial Association, the Air Line Pilots Association, and the Professional Air Traffic Controllers Organization. Nevertheless, polls showed that Reagan made deep inroads among blue-collar workers. Reagan broke even with Carter among blue-collar workers in general, lost among union families by only 5 to 7 percentage points (in comparison to a 27 percentage point win by Carter among these voters in 1976), and actually won a plurality among white union voters.[9]

Press reaction to the election results emphasized the breadth of Reagan's victory and the historical character of the Senate change. The *Washington Post* proclaimed 1980 to be "the most astonishing landslide in election history."[10] Reagan's landslide and congressional coattails still dominated thinking in Washington when the PATCO strike began.

Reagan's election and the year that followed were framed by several national challenges that would interact with the PATCO strike. In the eyes of most Americans, and of Reagan himself, the chief of these were economic. For nearly half a century before 1981, public economics was dominated by varying forms of Keynesianism, the school of thought holding that the key to economic prosperity was government manipulation of aggregate demand through fiscal policy. The challenge of the 1970s was that the economy began delivering high inflation and recession at the same time, a phenomenon that became known as "stagflation" unanticipated by Keynesian theory. From 1977 through 1980, the most common measure of the Consumer Price Index came in at

6.7 percent, 9.0 percent, 13.3 percent, and 12.5 percent. At the same time, recession took hold in 1979–80, leading to a high unemployment rate of 7.8 percent nationally and Depression-level devastation in some industrial towns such as Flint, Michigan and Toledo, Ohio.[11] At the same time, productivity fell and real family incomes in 1980 suffered their worst decline since World War II. Voters resoundingly declared inflation the most important issue of the 1980 election.[12]

Reagan, most other Republican officeholders, and many Democrats blamed excessive federal spending and resulting deficits for inflation. From 1965 to 1980, federal spending had increased from $118 billion to $591 billion. In inflation-adjusted dollars, spending had almost doubled. Deficits had grown from $1 billion to $74 billion, in real dollars an increase of about fifty-two times. Most was driven by domestic spending, as the share of the federal budget represented by defense spending fell from 43 percent to 23 percent.[13] The first point in Reagan's five-point economic program, announced on the campaign trail in September 1980, was "Controlling the rate of growth of federal spending to reasonable, prudent levels." The other four were to reduce the tax burden, reduce the regulatory burden, assure a stable money supply, and return confidence by hewing to a consistent policy.[14]

A second major set of problems was found abroad. The 1970s were widely seen as a decade of American retreat in the face of Communist and jihadist enemies. (In fact, in mid-1979 conservative Democrat Ben Wattenberg wrote a piece for the *New York Times Magazine*, reprinted in *Reader's Digest*, entitled "It's Time to Stop America's Retreat."[15]) Starting with the fall of Saigon in April 1975, the Soviet empire had incorporated an additional ten countries, or an average of one every six months: South Vietnam, Cambodia, and Laos in Indochina; Angola and Mozambique in southern Africa; Ethiopia and South Yemen on the Horn of Africa; Nicaragua and Grenada in the Caribbean basin; and finally Afghanistan, pointed at the strategic Persian Gulf region. It was the Soviet invasion of Afghanistan in December 1979 that definitively brought the illusions of détente crashing down.

At the same time, US military readiness was exposed as dangerously lacking, leading US Army General Edward Meyer to refer to the "hollow Army" in congressional testimony, and the Islamist revolution in

Iran in 1979, led by the Ayatollah Ruhollah Khomeini, converted a stalwart friend of the United States into a bitter enemy. Khomeini's regime held US diplomatic personnel hostage for 444 days, releasing them on Reagan's inauguration day. A military rescue mission launched by Carter had failed disastrously in April 1980. American credibility was in question globally, a potentially hazardous state of affairs in a dangerous world with adversaries as varied as Khomeini, the Soviet Politburo, Libya's Moammar Khadafy, and Cuba's Fidel Castro, among others. As the new US president, Reagan's actions would be noticed, not just by Americans, but by both friends and foes looking for a clue about what sort of man he was. Did he possess resolve, or could he be rolled?

At the same time Reagan had to consider the possibility that submitting to the air controllers might provide an undesirable lesson to adversaries abroad, the controllers also looked beyond American borders. In the summer of 1980, Polish ship workers in Gdansk began an independent union called Solidarity. Though proclaiming themselves to be "workers' paradises," the socialist states of the Soviet bloc prohibited such independent expressions of the workers' interests, and tensions in Poland grew in the remainder of 1980 and throughout 1981 until the Polish regime declared martial law, arresting Solidarity's leadership in December. Naturally, the anti-Communist Reagan took up the cause of Solidarity and warned the Soviets against intervention. For their part, Joseph A. McCartin notes, "Unionists often compared PATCO to Lech Walesa's *Solidarnosc* (Solidarity) movement.... Reagan had repeatedly championed the right of the Poles to strike against their government, the argument went. How could he deny American workers 'the same basic right'?"[16] The difference, arguably, was that the Poles lived in a Communist dictatorship where all large-scale enterprises were owned by the state. In Poland, unlike in the United States, if there was no right to strike against the government there was no right to strike at all. Nevertheless, many in the union movement accepted the analogy and hoped the parallel might compel the administration to accept a strike.

A third American challenge was institutional in character. Many Americans had come to fear that the presidency had grown incapable of decisive action, that the office was "too big for one man." When Reagan took office in 1981, the last successful president had been Dwight

D. Eisenhower, who had departed the White House two decades earlier. John F. Kennedy had died less than three years into his term, having accomplished little of his agenda; Lyndon Johnson obtained passage of most of his expansive agenda, but his policies failed in Vietnam (and, many argued, in the war on poverty as well); Richard Nixon was forced to resign in disgrace under threat of impeachment; Gerald Ford, the "accidental president," lost the bid to be elected in his own right after a little more than two years in office; and Jimmy Carter was a one-term president defeated in a landslide. The presidency, which had once appeared imperial, now appeared incapable. It seemed possible that no one could fulfill its promise, and some suggested radical constitutional changes such as a single long term, multiple presidents, or congressional terms that would be aligned with presidential terms to increase cooperation between the branches.[17] In 1980, noted presidential scholar Richard E. Neustadt asked "Is the presidency possible?"[18] Scholars Michael Nelson and Sidney Milkis likewise noted that "It seemed during the final days of the Carter administration that the presidency no longer worked, that presidents had become frustrated beyond hope of achievement."[19] When he took office, it was an open question whether Reagan would be up to the challenge.

The key to Reagan's ability to address all three challenges can be found in Richard E. Neustadt's seminal work on the presidency. In *Presidential Power*, Neustadt distinguishes between a president's *powers*—his constitutional or legal authority to command troops, veto legislation, and make appointments, for example—and his *power*—his practical ability to get things done. The former changed little from president to president, and even less within the space of a presidency. Yet presidents' ability to achieve what they wanted varied dramatically, even within a single presidency. The president's *power* was largely informal and fluid. It depended on the president's ability to persuade members of Congress, bureaucrats, and others. His ability to persuade them depended on his reputation for strength, reliable follow-through, and capacity to move the public and hence to confer benefits on friends and exact costs on those who obstruct him. Ultimately, Neustadt says, the president's public standing and his professional reputation would be decisive.[20] As Reagan's presidency unfolded, and as the PATCO crisis developed, it was clear that Reagan and his advisers were deeply aware of the dynamic at the heart of Neustadt's analysis.

The Reagan Administration: January 20 to August 3, 1981

When Reagan took office on January 20, 1981, he laid out his view of government. His inaugural address touched on themes that would intersect with the PATCO strike less than seven months later:

> In this present crisis, government is not the solution to our problem; government is the problem. . . .
>
> We hear much of special interest groups. Well, our concern must be for a special interest group that has been too long neglected. It knows no sectional boundaries or ethnic and racial divisions, and it crosses political party lines. It is made up of men and women who raise our food, patrol our streets, man our mines and factories, teach our children, keep our homes, and heal us when we're sick—professionals, industrialists, shopkeepers, clerks, cabbies, and truck drivers. They are, in short, "We the people," this breed called Americans. . . .
>
> We are a nation that has a government—not the other way around. And this makes us special among the nations of the Earth. Our government has no power except that granted it by the people. It is time to check and reverse the growth of government, which shows signs of having grown beyond the consent of the governed. . . .
>
> It is no coincidence that our present troubles parallel and are proportionate to the intervention and intrusion in our lives that result from unnecessary and excessive growth of government. . . .
>
> It is time to reawaken this industrial giant, to get government back within its means, and to lighten our punitive tax burden. And these will be our first priorities, and on these principles there will be no compromise.[21]

Reagan's first priority was to secure congressional passage of his economic program, which consisted of tax and spending cuts meant to implement the vision of government outlined in his inaugural address. This required enactment of two large and complicated pieces of legislation that proceeded from an overall budget resolution specifying levels of expenditure, levels of revenue, and projected deficits. Once Reagan had secured the difficult passage of a budget resolution slashing billions of dollars in spending and calling for a significant tax cut, detailed legislation had to be written to execute the resolution.

On the spending side, this took the form of the Omnibus Budget Reconciliation Act of 1981. OBRA, as it was called, ended up containing $36 billion of spending cuts in fiscal year 1982 and $140 billion over three years. Although these spending "cuts" were measured not against current spending but against anticipated future spending, they were nevertheless the largest such reductions since the advent of the New Deal welfare state. Touching on dozens of domestic programs, every one of which had a constituency, OBRA was widely seen as, at best, a tough sell to Congress. Opposed by the Democratic House leadership, which offered a less robust alternative, OBRA ultimately prevailed after weeks of intensive personal lobbying by the president. Almost every Republican member of the House and Senate supported the measure, as did dozens of moderate and conservative Democrats.

On the tax side, Reagan's original proposal was built around the supply-side bill introduced in the previous Congress by Congressman Jack Kemp and Senator William Roth. Kemp-Roth had envisioned a 30 percent across-the-board individual income tax cut over three years (10–10–10). The administration bill that ultimately emerged (the Economic Recovery Tax Act, or ERTA) cut income taxes by 25 percent across three years (5–10–10), included faster depreciation for business investments, and would index income tax rates to inflation starting in 1984, significantly limiting the "bracket creep" which had driven millions of taxpayers into higher tax brackets due to only nominal increases in income. Again, Democratic leaders offered an alternative, and a bidding war ensued which added billions in special tax breaks. In the end, Reagan won the bidding war, too, and his tax cut passed.[22] These demonstrations of Reagan's legislative prowess peaked exactly as the PATCO strike loomed. OBRA passed the House on June 26 and the Senate on July 13; the conference committee report was approved in both houses of Congress on July 31. ERTA passed the House on July 29 and the Senate on July 31. The final ERTA conference committee report was approved by the Senate on August 3, the first day of the strike, and on the following day in the House. Only the original OBRA vote in the House was even close; ERTA passed 323–107 in the House and by a voice vote in the Senate.

Throughout, Reagan mobilized supporters of his approach through effective rhetoric. He appeared before a joint session of Congress to pitch his plan on February 18, then again on April 28. Three months later, as the tax battle heated up in Congress, he appeared on national television from the Oval Office, appealing to Americans to contact their congressional representatives. The response was unusually strong as congressional offices were deluged with supportive phone calls and telegrams; ever since, presidents have tried but failed to match Reagan's success.[23] Reagan's public rhetorical offensive was complemented by an aggressive inside strategy aimed at identifying those senators and representatives who could be swayed and talking with them, sometimes by phone but often in person at the White House.[24]

Contributing to Reagan's success was his response to the first real crisis of his presidency, the attempt on his life made on March 30 by John Hinckley Jr. Despite the severity of his wound—Reagan lost more than half of his blood as a bullet collapsed a lung and was lodged less than an inch from his heart—the president showed resilience and good humor, joking to his wife Nancy, "Honey, I forgot to duck," and to his assembled surgical team, "I hope you are Republicans."[25] Good wishes flowed into the White House from Americans of all political persuasions, who had been kept blissfully unaware of the seriousness of the president's wounds, and his approval in the Gallup poll rose from 60 percent to 67 percent. When Reagan made his second appearance before a joint session of Congress a few weeks later, he was met with thunderous applause.

The Brewing Conflict: The Rise of PATCO

The intersection of PATCO's course with Reagan the political juggernaut was a long time coming. Private sector unions had achieved tremendous breakthroughs in the 1930s, first in the collective bargaining requirements of the National Industrial Recovery Act of 1933, and then more permanently, in the National Labor Relations Act (or "Wagner

Act") of 1935. Membership in the American Federation of Labor (AFL), Congress of Industrial Organizations (CIO), and independent unions grew dramatically over the next two decades, reaching more than one-third of the private sector workforce by 1953. However, both Democratic and Republican officeholders of the period were opposed to public sector strikes. When then-governor Calvin Coolidge broke the Boston police strike in 1919, president Woodrow Wilson agreed with Coolidge, declaring the walkout "an intolerable crime against civilization."[26] Herbert Hoover also opposed public sector strikes. For his part, Franklin Roosevelt, who signed the Wagner Act and championed private sector unionism, declared that "Meticulous attention must be paid to the special relations and obligations of public servants to the public itself and to the government.... The process of collective bargaining, as usually understood, cannot be transplanted into the public service."[27] More to the point, "A strike of public employees manifests nothing less than an attempt on their part to obstruct the operations of government until their demands are satisfied. Such action looking toward the paralysis of government by those who have sworn to support it is unthinkable and intolerable."[28]

Consequently, until the late 1950s the right of public employees to form unions or engage in collective bargaining was not recognized by law at any level of government. New York City was the first major city to do so in 1958, and the next year Wisconsin became the first state to recognize public employee unions. Partly to repay organized labor for its crucial assistance in his 1960 presidential campaign and partly to forestall more radical legislation in Congress, President John F. Kennedy signed Executive Order 10988 in 1962 giving federal employees the right to organize. Some were also allowed to engage in what amounted to collective bargaining, though the term was avoided. The final wording of the order was the result of a ferocious struggle inside the administration and did not meet all of organized labor's demands. However, AFL-CIO head George Meany praised the executive order as a "Wagner Act for public employees,"[29] and it inspired a wave of unionization across all levels of government for the next two decades.[30] In 1961, only about one in ten government workers were unionized; by 1976, about 40 percent were.[31]

Even as organization of public employees spread, however, public employee strikes remained illegal. Several arguments were made to justify the prohibition. One was that striking against government was, as Franklin Roosevelt contended, a strike against the people themselves and against the government's fundamental sovereignty. Another was that government provides essential services that cannot be discontinued without inflicting or risking serious harm on society. A third was that, while strikes in the private sector can be kept within reasonable confines by market forces, governments are not bound by market forces.[32] These arguments, however valid they may have been, did not prevent a wave of "job actions"—work slowdowns, "sickouts," or outright strikes—by public employee unions in the 1970s.

Some air traffic controllers began to informally discuss the desirability of organizing for reforms after a deadly mid-air collision over New York in December 1960. Many controllers believed the Federal Aviation Agency had whitewashed the role of a dysfunctional air traffic control system in the collision. Two of the key figures in this discussion were Mike Rock and Jack Maher. Maher and Rock both came to the FAA by way of comparable military experience, and both came from blue-collar union families.[33] Though they did not yet know each other well, they were both on duty at the same New York air traffic control center at the time of the 1960 midair collision. The first instrument they chose for their efforts was the Air Traffic Control Association (ATCA), which had been formed in 1956 and had recruited more than half the FAA controllers as members by the early 1960s. ATCA was not an advocacy group for the controllers, but rather was dominated by FAA officials within the governing council. Efforts to turn ATCA into a tool for constructive criticism, reform, and advocacy of controllers' interests failed.[34]

After EO 10988 was promulgated in 1962, controllers sought other opportunities for representation. Initially, a number of labor organizations worked to recruit members from among air traffic controllers. In the mid-1960s, the most successful of these was the National Association of Government Employees (NAGE), an independent union that harshly criticized the FAA and demanded that controllers be allowed to retire after 20 years. NAGE surged ahead of ATCA in membership. Reeling under the criticism, the FAA promised to pay overtime and hire six hundred new controllers, but Congress did not authorize the necessary funds. Ultimately, NAGE fell short of controllers' hopes, as it was a general government employees union with no particular focus on controllers or their issues.

In 1966 and 1967, controllers in Chicago and Los Angeles made the decision locally to engage in work slowdowns. These so-called work-to-rule actions, in which controllers followed regulations precisely rather than utilizing commonly accepted shortcuts that moved air traffic more efficiently, eventually resulted in wage concessions from the FAA. In the wake of these successes, controllers in the New York area, led by Maher and Rock, formed the Metropolitan Controllers Association (MCA), the first regional controllers organization. In December 1967, they pitched a proposal to create an air controllers subdivision to the NAGE leadership, but controllers found them unresponsive, if not hostile, to the idea.

Having concluded that they needed to form their own organization, Maher and Rock recruited famed attorney F. Lee Bailey to headline an organizational meeting in New York on January 11, 1968. More than seven hundred controllers from twenty-two states attended, and the Professional Air Traffic Controllers Organization was born, with Maher its first national coordinator and Rock as the chairman of its board of directors. Initially, it was unclear whether PATCO, which avoided the use of the word "union" in its name, would be a professional association or an organization aggressively advocating for the controllers, as a union might. That decision was made six months later when a convention of the new organization voted to bar supervisors, a prerequisite for being recognized as a negotiating representative of the controllers under EO 10988.

Within a few weeks, PATCO engaged in its first "job action" against the FAA (which was now the Federal Aviation Administration, operating under the new federal Department of Transportation), a work slowdown of air traffic controllers in major cities including New York, Chicago, Denver, and Kansas City. After several weeks of snarled air traffic, Congress and the FAA conceded. Congress agreed to fund new controller positions and met PATCO's chief demand, which was an exemption of controllers from the federal government's restrictions on overtime pay. The FAA also agreed to dues checkoff for PATCO nationwide. The successful action was largely approved by both the public and the media, which seemed to have more sympathy for the controllers than for the sinking Johnson administration. It also led to significant growth in PATCO membership and to a practical confirmation that PATCO was going to act as a union rather than a congenial professional association. Not least, the confrontation between PATCO and the FAA changed the relationship between the two, rendering them permanently adversarial.

When the FAA dragged its heels on some of the promised reforms, PATCO took a step closer to a strike in June 1969 by calling a "sickout" (akin to the so-called Blue Flu among unionized police officers) at the Denver, Kansas City, and Houston centers, which quickly spread to New York and Chicago. The sickout disrupted air traffic even more than the previous year's work slowdown. After receiving informal assurances that some of their demands would be met, PATCO leaders called off the sickout. However, the FAA then asserted that no assurances had been given and retaliated by rescinding the dues checkoff agreement with PATCO and threatening to transfer key organizers. When a mediation committee voted in favor of PATCO's position on the transfers, the Department of Transportation refused to abide by it. In response, just before Easter 1970, PATCO began what amounted to the first centrally planned, though lightly disguised, nationwide strike by a public employee union in American history. This sickout lasted nineteen days, finally collapsing when courts began issuing restraining orders and imposing fines on strikers. The permanent injunctions issued by courts in 1970 would later play an important role in the 1981 strike.

Set back on its heels, the union regrouped by attaching itself to the Maritime Engineers Beneficial Association (MEBA), a small but politically connected AFL-CIO union. It also elected new leaders, making John F. Leyden of New York president and removing F. Lee Bailey as general counsel. As a result of Leyden's leadership and MEBA's assistance, in a little over two years PATCO had won three big victories: reinstatement of the organizers fired after the 1969 sickout, passage of a long-sought bill permitting controllers over fifty years of age to retire with full benefits after twenty years on the job, and Department of Labor clearance to seek recognition as the sole representative of controllers nationwide. In the summer of 1972, the representation election was held, and 84 percent of the ten thousand controllers who voted supported PATCO. The union was certified as the official representative of air traffic controllers nationwide, and dues checkoff resumed, providing the union with significant new resources.

This comeback was abetted by President Richard M. Nixon, who was endorsed by PATCO in his 1972 run against George McGovern. In 1969, Nixon had signed Executive Order 11491, which modified Kennedy's EO 10988 to facilitate further unionization of the federal work force. From 1970 to 1972, PATCO took full advantage of its terms. Then, in 1972, the anti-Communist labor leaders threatened to scuttle Nixon's grain deal with the Soviet Union by refusing to load the grain for shipment. To defuse this threat, Nixon authorized his labor deputy Charles Colson to do whatever necessary to placate the unions. In secret negotiations, MEBA obtained assurances regarding reinstatement of fired controllers and the president's willingness to sign the early retirement bill.[35]

In the half decade following these victories, PATCO emerged as the "most militant, most densely organized union" in the federal government.[36] Early successes included winning an increase in free flights for controllers (the so-called familiarization flights, or FAMs), introduction of a more hospitable grievance process, and creation of an air safety reporting mechanism, including amnesty for controllers who reported safety issues they had uncovered. As the decade progressed, though, the union found itself on the defensive. It won some additional concessions, but resorted to a work slowdown in late 1974 to prevent a rollback of the 1973 FAM benefit. More generally, federal law still prohibited negotiation over pay, and pay was becoming a crucial question. Inflation was rapidly eroding real wages, and the union was not legally permitted to raise the issue. To square this circle, Leyden and the union pushed for a reclassification of controllers by the Civil Service Commission based on increased air traffic since the last reclassification seven years earlier. When a draft report indicated that the CSC would recommend wholesale downgrading of controllers, a brief work slowdown had some effect. The final report upgraded controllers in many facilities and downgraded only one facility. About half of PATCO members would receive an increase in pay, but about half would not, distinctions that led to dissatisfaction and charges of "sellout."

In a new chapter of an old story, the FAA took its time implementing the reclassification, further strengthening the militant faction within PATCO. Under pressure from below, Leyden in 1977 supported creation of a PATCO "beneficial fund," which in reality was designed to serve as a strike fund. The threat of a job action pushed the FAA into additional concessions, and a three-year contract was reached in December 1977 that included additional controller training, broadened opportunities for arbitration, liberalized FAMs, and easier transfer to other regions. Leyden saw the contract as another (admittedly modest) incremental step on the path forward. The militants were not satisfied, though, and the contract passed the PATCO vote with only 62 percent in favor. Then the three largest international air carriers embarrassed Leyden by rebelling against the promised FAMs on international flights. Afraid that other parts of the agreement could be unraveled, Leyden and the PATCO board called for a work slowdown if the FAMs issue was not resolved.

However, many PATCO members were opposed to the slowdown or gave only tepid approval, seeing it as a risky job action in pursuit of an issue of marginal importance—not to mention, one difficult to justify to the public. Fewer controllers participated, and the effects on air travel were much less significant than earlier PATCO efforts. The slowdown quickly crumbled and PATCO gained nothing. By the end of 1978, the union had also lost provisions allowing early retirement due to medical conditions when a fraud scheme was uncovered, and a midair collision over San Diego led to the end of the immunity program won in 1975.

After the setbacks of 1978, a group of militant dissidents called the "Fifth Column movement" began meeting controllers around the country. In an attempt to capture (and co-opt) their energy, Leyden enlisted his vice president, Robert E. Poli, along with Jack Maher and Mike Rock, to organize preparations for an all-out strike if the next round of contract negotiations were not fruitful. Poli travelled the country, oversaw a network of strike organizers who called themselves the "Choirboys," and declared to supportive audiences of controllers, "The only illegal strike is an unsuccessful strike."[37] When Poli and the Choirboys became convinced that Leyden would never actually proceed with a strike, Poli informed Leyden he would be challenging him for the presidency of PATCO at the national convention in April 1980.

However, the conflict came to a premature boil at the PATCO board meeting in January 1980. After hours of mutual acrimony, Poli announced that he was resigning from the vice presidency to campaign independently. Leyden, facing a board that was mostly in Poli's corner, resigned, too. The board voted to accept Leyden's resignation and reject Poli's, thus making the latter president of PATCO as of February 1, 1980. Poli and his organization of militant Choirboys had prevailed, a triumph confirmed in the PATCO convention a few months later when he defeated George Kerr, Leyden's sole remaining supporter on the board. At the same PATCO convention, Congressman William Lacy Clay Sr. (D-MO) also stoked the appetite for a strike with an incendiary speech. Clay advised that the organization must "learn the rules of the game and learn them well." Those rules, according to Clay, were 1) "Don't put the interests of any other group ahead of your own," 2) *"You take what you can,* give up only what you must," and 3) *"You take it from whomever you can, whenever you can, however you can."*[38]

Throughout this period, the controllers had developed strong grievances against the FAA built around pay, mandatory overtime, aging equipment, and, perhaps most of all, FAA high-handedness and occasional duplicity. To observers, "The sense of dissatisfaction was deep and genuine, whether or not it was justified"—and independent studies both before and after the strike, such as the Corson Committee Report in 1970, the Rose Report in 1978, and the Johnson Report in 1982, indicated that at least some of it was justified.[39] It had been a decade since the Corson Committee Report had highlighted high rates of attrition among air traffic control specialists.[40] The Rose Report and subsequent congressional hearings in 1979 brought to the foreground additional concerns about the stresses faced by controllers. For example, the Rose Report revealed that controllers suffered from hypertension at rates 50 to 100 percent greater than other American men their ages, though it also included serious caveats in its findings.[41] More to the point, since 1969, the FAA had repeatedly made promises and then reneged. Most PATCO members seemed prepared to take the next step—an open, undisguised strike.

Poli's victory, though a win for supporters of a more aggressive stance by PATCO, carried costs with it. PATCO's valuable ally J. J. O'Donnell, head of the Air Line Pilots Association (ALPA), was dismayed, as was MEBA president Jesse Calhoon. And while Poli had prevailed at the convention, more than one-third of the delegates had voted for Kerr, including majorities at six of the biggest air control facilities (New York, Boston, Washington, Miami, Dallas-Fort Worth, and Chicago).

With new leadership fully committed to the strike plan, PATCO accelerated preparations for 1981. The FAA had also been preparing for a PATCO strike since 1978 and redoubled its efforts. In the fall of 1980, at the behest of FAA director Langhorne Bond, the Justice Department issued a warning against an illegal strike, and the FAA published a strike contingency plan in the *Federal Register*. In September 1980, FAA representatives and Poli appeared before a congressional hearing. The FAA presented evidence that PATCO was preparing for a strike; Poli denied it, flatly declaring that "this organization is not going to strike next year."[42]

By October 1, 1980, the PATCO leadership had settled on a set of demands for the next round of contract negotiations and mailed them to the union's members. The demands included:

- A $10,000 across-the-board raise for all controllers, equivalent to $33,000 in 2022
- An additional 10 percent raise the following year
- Cost of living adjustments that would subsequently raise controllers' pay by 1.5 percent for every 1 percent of inflation
- A four-day work week with three consecutive days off
- An increase in retirement benefits from half pay at twenty years to 75 percent pay at twenty years
- A 30 percent bonus for training hours[43]

Another major goal was to move air traffic controllers out of the civil service system altogether, making it legal for them to strike. The government estimated the overall cost of the package to be $1.1 billion in the first year.[44] It was a radical set of demands in an economic environment of stagflation, a political environment of retrenchment, and a legal environment in which strikes and negotiations regarding pay were prohibited.

Less than a month later, Poli and the PATCO Board endorsed Ronald Reagan for president. By PATCO's lights, Jimmy Carter had proven a profound disappointment. Along with the Teamsters and ALPA, MEBA had already endorsed Reagan. Before finalizing the endorsement, PATCO general counsel Richard Leighton sent a letter to Reagan's labor liaison Michael Balzano stipulating PATCO's six endorsement requirements and requesting a confirmation that Reagan was committed to them. The requirements were 1) removal of Langhorne Bond as FAA head, 2) consultation with PATCO in the selection of Bond's replacement, 3) upgrading of air traffic control equipment, 4) reduction of work hours, 5) full staffing of all air traffic control positions, and 6) satisfactory revision of the 1978 Civil Service Reform Act, which had strengthened anti-strike provisions for federal employees.[45] Reagan responded with a letter that expressed general support for PATCO's goals without committing himself to them in detail. In the letter, Reagan acknowledged "the deplorable state of our nation's air traffic control system" and pledged that "my administration will work very closely with you to bring about a spirit of cooperation." Reagan further assured Poli that "if I am elected president, I will take whatever steps necessary to provide our air traffic controllers with the most modern equipment available and to adjust staff levels and work days so that they are commensurate with achieving a maximum degree of public safety."[46] (See Appendix B for the full text of Reagan's letter.) Poli and other PATCO leaders read between the lines and believed what they wanted to believe. In the view of Joseph A. McCartin, "The result was that when Reagan cruised to a smashing victory over Jimmy Carter on November 4, 1980, controllers' expectations of what they might be able to get from his administration rose to levels profoundly out of sync with the political realities of the moment."[47]

Altogether, since its formation, PATCO had engaged in a month-long slowdown in 1968, a three-day slowdown in 1969, a twenty-day sickout by 2,200 controllers in 1970, a five-day slowdown at the busiest airports in 1976, two brief slowdowns at major airports in 1978, and a highly disruptive one-day slowdown at Chicago O'Hare in 1980.[48] In the words of law professors Bernard D. Meltzer and Cass R. Sunstein, during those episodes, executive enforcement of the no-strike law had been "so lax and erratic as to approach a de facto recognition of 'illegal' public employee strikes as a regular part of the negotiating process."[49] (Also relevant to PATCO's aspirations, the Nixon Administration had tolerated and settled a major postal workers strike in 1970.) Criminal law was not invoked, almost no strikers lost their jobs, and PATCO had shown that it could inflict serious losses on the airlines and the nation. On the other hand, federal courts had imposed injunctions that could be quite costly for the union if a strike lasted too long.

The relationship between air traffic controllers and the FAA was as contentious as ever, an animosity to which both sides had contributed. PATCO, which had grown increasingly militant since its formation twelve years earlier, was poised to test the limits of the new president's support. The stage was set for the strike of 1981 and the decisions that helped define a presidency.

CHAPTER 2

The Cast of Characters

In the end, the decisions about how to deal with the PATCO strike were Ronald Reagan's to make. Although he was the lead character, he was far from the only person involved. As the crisis moved toward a culmination, a wide-ranging cast worked with Reagan in the administration and within processes established by him and his top advisers. At the same time, PATCO had its key actors, and individuals outside the direct parameters of the conflict still helped to shape it.

The Reagan Administration

Aside from the president himself, the two most prominent figures on the PATCO issue in the Reagan administration were Secretary of Transportation Drew Lewis and Federal Aviation Administration Director J. Lynn Helms. Both were appointed by the president and confirmed by the Senate. In the chain of command, Lewis was Helms's superior, as the FAA was a unit of the Transportation Department. Moreover, unlike in previous negotiating rounds, the secretary of transportation would ultimately take the lead and personally participate in negotiations. The FAA director, though rarely participating directly in the negotiations, continued to play an important advisory role. Moreover, Helms was primarily responsible for strengthening and then executing the FAA's strike contingency plan, a critical component of Reagan's response.

A graduate of Haverford College and Harvard Business School, Drew Lewis was "generally regarded here as the most able domestic

Cabinet officer in the administration."[1] He had worked in private industry, including a nine-year stint as trustee of the bankrupt Reading Railroad, and had gained "a reputation for wizardry in the art of the corporate turnaround."[2] Lewis became involved in Republican politics in the 1960s when he managed the US House and Senate campaigns of Richard Schweiker. He had made his own foray into electoral politics in the Watergate year of 1974, when he ran a credible race for governor of Pennsylvania but ultimately lost. Lewis then chaired the Pennsylvania presidential campaign of Gerald Ford in 1976 and led the Pennsylvania delegation to the 1976 Republican National Convention in Kansas City. When Reagan tried to pry away Ford's Pennsylvania delegates by declaring he would make Senator Schweiker his running mate, Lewis held firm and kept the delegation in line for Ford. Impressed, Reagan called on Lewis and made him the Reagan chair in Pennsylvania in 1980. Lewis was described as "among the two or three most powerful Republicans in Pennsylvania and one of the most powerful in the Northeast."[3] He went on to become the deputy political director of the 1980 Reagan-Bush campaign committee.

By all accounts, Lewis was of a moderate and pragmatic temperament. In the view of labor historian Joseph A. McCartin, "Lewis thought PATCO's demands and its claims of overwork and underpay were grossly inflated, but he believed that an agreement could be reached if pragmatism prevailed on both sides of the bargaining table during the 1981 negotiations. He was the best negotiating partner PATCO could have hoped for from the Reagan administration."[4]

Helms, the FAA director, was a former Marine Corps fighter pilot who had little use for PATCO and gave even less credence than Lewis to its claims of woe. The son of a railroad brakeman, he attended college on an ROTC scholarship, flew combat missions in the Korean War, and then trained test pilots. In 1956 he entered the defense aeronautics industry before moving on to head Piper, a small-plane manufacturer. At Piper, he came to disdain unions, which he thought were threatening to make the company uncompetitive, and hoped to move his operations from a unionized to a non-unionized state. Referring to PATCO's salary demands, Helms said "Go and get yourself a guitar and be a rock and roll singer, and then you can make that kind of money."[5]

In his letter to Reagan outlining PATCO's conditions for an endorsement, union general counsel Leighton insisted that the prospective Reagan administration offer the union an opportunity for input over the next FAA director, or even a veto if it deemed the choice unacceptable. Documentary evidence seems to show that Reagan's people did run Helms's name by PATCO and, rather surprisingly, received no objection.[6]

While Lewis and Helms were the two most central administration figures, many others were also important. Besides Lewis, the other cabinet officer directly involved was William French Smith, attorney general of the United States, who had been with Reagan since the California days. He hailed from an old New England family, and a distant ancestor had been president of Harvard University. He went west to get his bachelor's degree at UCLA, then upon completion of his Harvard law degree returned to California to take a position in the high-powered Los Angeles law firm of Gibson, Dunn & Crutcher. He was one among a group of elite Californians who urged Reagan to run for governor in 1966, and the two became close friends. In 1968, Governor Reagan appointed Smith, who was by then a part of Reagan's famous "kitchen cabinet" of informal advisers, to the University of California Board of Regents, where Smith served three terms as chair. He was a senior partner at Gibson, Dunn & Crutcher when Reagan appointed him attorney general after the 1980 election.[7] Smith would have the crucial job of providing legal advice to the president and leading the Justice Department into action when necessary.

A second set of Reagan administration figures were less central to the drama but nevertheless important. These were economic advisers Martin Anderson and David Stockman. Stockman was the 34-year-old director of the Office of Management and Budget (OMB). In his short life, he had experienced a number of transformations—from a high school fan of Barry Goldwater, to an activist in the far-left Students for a Democratic Society while at Michigan State University, to a student at Harvard Divinity School—before finally coming under the influence of Daniel Patrick Moynihan, James Q. Wilson, and Nathan Glazer. In 1972 he went to work for liberal Republican Congressman John Anderson of Illinois, where he eventually came under the wing of supply-side hero

Jack Kemp. Stockman was elected from Michigan as one of the youngest members of the House of Representatives in 1976. During his short time in Congress, he attained a reputation as a dogged budget and tax cutter. In 1980, Stockman grabbed the attention of Ronald Reagan by serving as a highly effective stand-in for John Anderson and Jimmy Carter in Reagan's debate preparation. Reagan appointed him OMB director and elevated his position to cabinet status. Stockman was responsible for putting together Reagan's 1981 spending plan that ended up cutting $36 billion in domestic programs from a federal budget that spent about $680 billion in fiscal year 1981. Often described as the administration's "wonder boy," Stockman was a forceful spokesman for the Reagan budget and shared the glory when the plan was adopted by Congress in July 1981. A 1981 *New York Times* profile called Stockman the "cutting edge" of Reagan's economic revolution. "Overnight," the *Times* observed, "this young, relatively obscure, two-term Michigan Congressman has attained a position of astonishing power."[8] Although his luster would diminish before the end of year when an interview in *The Atlantic* revealed his own doubts about the plan and the president, Stockman was at the peak of his prestige as PATCO hurtled toward a strike. As a budget hawk, he was no fan of PATCO's substantial salary demands or of the probable fiscal impact of opening the floodgates to federal employee union demands more generally.

Parallel to Stockman as the director of the OMB, Donald J. Devine served as Reagan's director of the Office of Personnel Management (OPM). As such, his responsibilities included oversight of the overall federal employment system. He took a keen interest in the prospect of any federal employee strike, and he understood that the precedent set in PATCO negotiations would reverberate throughout the government. Devine was widely judged one of the most visible OPM directors ever and was referred to in his official OPM biography as "President Reagan's chief advisor on Federal civil service personnel matters." Tasked with slimming down the federal bureaucracy, Devine was labelled Reagan's "terrible swift sword of the civil service" and "the man federal workers love to hate" by the *Washington Post*.[9] Raised in Brooklyn and with a Syracuse PhD, he was a veteran of the 1976 and 1980 Reagan presidential campaigns, and he was an associate professor of government and political science at the University of Maryland in March 1981 when tapped to head OPM.[10]

Several figures in the White House also played important roles, starting with Martin Anderson, who served as assistant to the president for policy development in economic and domestic policy. The son of a dairy farmer and a nurse, Anderson had been an academic prodigy, earning a Dartmouth BA on a scholarship, two master's degrees, a PhD, and promotion to associate professor at Columbia Business School by the age of twenty-eight. He then advised Richard Nixon's 1968 campaign and his presidential administration, playing a key role in Nixon's policy decision to end military conscription and move to an all-volunteer army. Anderson's economic interests were wide-ranging, and he served as the only full-time economic adviser to Ronald Reagan's 1976 and 1980 presidential campaigns, taking the lead in the development and release of the campaign's five-part economic plan in September 1980. He followed Reagan to the White House after the election, reporting to presidential counselor Edwin Meese.[11] In that capacity, he was sometimes called "the conscience of the administration" for ensuring policies remained consistent with Reagan's campaign promises and views.[12] In Anderson's view, inflation was the number one threat to the economic health of the nation, and federal spending was the number one cause of inflation.[13]

The young Craig Fuller (who turned thirty in 1981) was another Californian who had begun in Reagan's gubernatorial staff. In 1981, he served Reagan as the secretary of the cabinet. As a *New York Times* profile noted in 1985, Fuller's position was "a role central to keeping the White House bureaucracy running smoothly." In that role, he gained a reputation as "a skillful infighter and as tough but not abrasive."[14] During the PATCO crisis, Fuller's task would be to monitor the progress of negotiations and manage the flow of information into the White House.

Reagan's White House labor liaison Robert Bonitati connected with US Senator Howard Baker's election campaign while a graduate student at the University of Tennessee, and subsequently he became Baker's chief of staff in 1967. After leaving the Senate office, he headed the government affairs office for the Air Line Pilots Association (ALPA) for six years, giving him familiarity with labor issues in the aviation realm. During the 1980 Reagan campaign, Bonitati served as a liaison to labor and was critical in brokering PATCO's Reagan endorsement. Once Reagan was sworn in, Bonitati continued in this role as special assistant to the president.[15] Having been a point of contact with PATCO during the campaign, Bonitati remained a secondary channel of communication during the negotiations and strike crisis.

Other White House advisers were instrumental to various facets of Reagan's interaction with the American public. Richard Wirthlin had been with Reagan for over a decade. With a Berkeley PhD and a professorship in economics at Brigham Young University, Wirthlin had started a polling firm in the 1960s. One of his clients was Barry Goldwater when he ran to regain his US Senate seat from Arizona in 1968. Goldwater referred Wirthlin to Reagan, who was then governor of California. Wirthlin became Reagan's pollster and public opinion adviser for the next twenty years, until Reagan left the White House. It was his job, Wirthlin later said, not to tell Reagan what he should do but to help him find the most effective way of explaining what he already wanted to do.[16]

On the other hand, David Gergen was a relative newcomer to the Reagan team. A native of North Carolina, Gergen graduated Yale and Harvard Law School, after which he spent four years in the United States Navy. He served Richard Nixon as the head of his speechwriting team. Gerald Ford elevated Gergen to the position of White House communications director before Gergen was named to the same position by Ronald Reagan in 1981. Like James Baker, Gergen was on George H. W. Bush's campaign staff in 1980 before being picked up by the Reagan White House.[17] His job would be to advise the president regarding communication on the PATCO issue.

The final set of relevant Reagan administration figures were the three men who shared the role of gatekeeper and confidant usually consolidated in the single chief of staff position: James Baker III, chief of staff; Michael Deaver, deputy chief of staff (with primary responsibility in public relations); and Edwin Meese III, counselor to the president, serving as the chief policy coordinator. This layer of advisers was farthest from the PATCO action, but they were the closest to Reagan and provided input as the crisis drew toward a culmination. As a unit, they were sometimes referred to as "The Troika," but they were quite varied in background, outlook, and temperament. Journalist Dom Bonafede described this arrangement as "the most extraordinary aspect of Reagan's executive structure."[18]

Meese and Deaver had been with Reagan since his California days; Baker had run the 1980 presidential campaign of George H. W. Bush, Reagan's strongest Republican competitor. Baker and Deaver were known for their more moderate political tendencies; Meese was the strongest conservative and (like Martin Anderson, who reported to him) saw his task being to "let Reagan be Reagan." Deaver, unlike Meese or Baker, had a close friendship with First Lady Nancy Reagan and consequently had a second avenue to the president's ear. As a result of these differences, the relationship among the Troika was sometimes strained. However, the arrangement also ensured that the president had access to a variety of voices and usually worked itself out in productive ways.

Operationally, the Troika had breakfast alone every morning, followed by a meeting with senior White House staff to provide orders for the day, followed by a meeting with the president in the Oval Office at around 9 a.m. At the end of the day, they would meet again with the president. The three agreed that no one but the director of the Central Intelligence Agency and the attorney general would be allowed to meet with Reagan unless at least one of them was present.[19]

Organization and Processes of the Administration

From his days as governor of California, Reagan had developed a style of management that organized his administration's work. As Dom Bonafede explains, "During his gubernatorial tenure, Reagan displayed a collegial administrative style that carried over into his presidency. He preferred to surround himself with familiar faces and to delegate action, leaving him free to oversee policy and deal with major decisions. He tolerated opposing points of view from his advisers but was uncomfortable with intramural acrimony."[20] Reagan later described it in the following "common sense" way:

1) Select the best people I could find from business and elsewhere.
2) Set policies and goals and do whatever I could to help them achieve those goals.

3) Encourage everyone in the group to share their views regardless of specialization.
4) When the discussion was over, they all knew it was up to me and me alone to make the decision.
5) Throughout the process, keep informed and make myself available for fine-tuning. However, do not micromanage. Don't interfere as long as the people you have picked are doing what you have in mind. A chief executive should not peer constantly over the shoulders of the people who are in charge of a project and tell them every few minutes what to do.[21]

Reagan's domestic policy advisor Martin Anderson would later write of his management style that "When it works, it is spectacular. When it fails, it is also spectacular."[22] A key element was to remain informed throughout the decision-making process; on occasions when Reagan failed to do so, such as the Iran-Contra affair, it was costly.

Reagan, like all presidents, grappled with the question of how to maximize his influence over the vast federal bureaucracy without overcentralizing and micromanaging. By instinct, he preferred "cabinet government:" pick good cabinet secretaries and give them freedom to operate. But Richard Nixon had utilized this model in his first term, and it had proven too subject to bureaucratic capture and too impervious to presidential direction. In his second term, Nixon centralized decision-making in the White House but became too isolated. Reagan combined the two modes, giving a larger role to the White House and the Office of Management and Budget to serve as the president's policy gatekeepers, while also relying on an adaptation of cabinet government. The secretaries would be important, but the White House, acting through the Office of Personnel Management, would take the lead in filling with Reagan loyalists the subcabinet—the crucial deputy and assistant secretaries and lower appointed positions—rather than leaving those positions for the secretaries to fill.[23] According to scholars Peter M. Benda and Charles H. Levine, "From the outset, the Reagan administration pursued a campaign to maximize presidential control over the federal bureaucracy that was more self-conscious in design and execution, and more comprehensive in scope, than that of any other administration of the modern era."[24]

PATCO Players

On the other side of the table, we have already been introduced to the new PATCO president, Robert E. Poli, who ascended to the leadership of the union in January 1980. Poli was raised in a blue-collar home in Pittsburgh, a big union town, and became an air traffic controller in the Air Force. Upon discharge, he went to work as a controller for the FAA at first the Pittsburgh and then the Cleveland air traffic control centers. From Cleveland Center he challenged the sitting PATCO vice president, defeating and replacing Bob Greene in 1972. As vice president, Poli long had a fruitful relationship with President John Leyden. In 1978, Leyden gave Poli responsibility for organizing the "Choirboys," the informal committee of PATCO militants preparing the union for a 1981 strike. However, Poli turned on Leyden when he and the Choirboys concluded that the president was unlikely to pull the trigger on a nationwide strike. Once the union was organized along militant lines, Poli and the organization adopted a symbiotic relationship; Poli served as the voice of the militants in the union, and the militants elevated him to the presidency. His strengths were organization and internal coalition building. However, his attachment to the militant wing and his rejection of Leyden's incrementalism would come at a heavy price: the ultimate destruction of PATCO.[25] Poli—a man who was "impatient and moved to immediate action rather than working through the established processes for communication and problem resolution"[26]—was convinced that a strike was probably inevitable and that PATCO would hold the high cards. He would be primarily responsible for executing the PATCO negotiating strategy.

Most of the remaining PATCO leadership also came from the more militant wing of the union. For example, Central Regional Vice President Gary Eads, thirty-seven, out of Kansas City Center was a crucial figure cut from the same cloth. He backed the Fifth Column movement and was an early supporter of Poli's candidacy. After the collapse of the strike, Eads would replace Poli as the union's last president. Robert E. Meyer, executive vice president, was another driving force behind the PATCO strategy. Meyer was, by certain measures, more moderate than Eads, having agonized over casting the decisive vote against Leyden at the January 1980 board meeting that deposed him.[27] Nevertheless, Meyer thought that he had found the key to guaranteeing a successful strike: bringing the Canadian Air Traffic Control Association (CATCA) into the fight by convincing the Canadian controllers that American skies were unsafe. Meyer calculated that a boycott of American flights by CATCA, possibly abetted by other controller associations abroad, could cut off transatlantic travel entirely. The government would be forced to give in.[28]

Two other key PATCO players would be notable by their absence: Mike Rock, sometimes known as "Mike Strike," and Jack Maher, both of whom had been instrumental in the organization of the controllers from the beginning. By 1980, Maher had spent a dozen years as PATCO's top strategist. At that time, he had a falling out with Poli and left the organization. Rock remained in PATCO, but was downgraded by the new leadership; he had served on the union's contract negotiating committee for each of its first three negotiations, but Poli excluded him in 1980 in favor of younger activists.[29] Thus, like Schrodinger's cat, two of the leading figures in the creation and development of PATCO both were and were not key actors in the 1981 strike. The union was largely following their strike plan, and the two continued to carry informal influence among many members; but they had either left the scene (Maher) or were not central figures in the negotiations (Rock).

On the Outside

While Reagan, other administration officials, and PATCO leaders were the primary actors in the drama, both the administration and PATCO had counterparts outside the negotiations.

The governmental counterparts to the executive branch were found in the other two branches of the federal government: Congress and the judiciary. Congress possessed both the power of legislation and the power of the purse. It was Congress that had formulated the laws prohibiting strikes by public employees and limiting the subjects of collective bargaining. Any broadening of public sector union rights at the federal level, as well as any contract concessions that cost money, would have to be enacted by Congress.

Congress, of course, is perpetually fragmented, with 435 members in the House and one hundred in the Senate (barring vacancies). In 1981, the institution was also just getting accustomed to a situation that had not happened since 1931–1932: a (nominally) Democratic House alongside a Republican Senate. Though congressional power was widely spread, one member of Congress was particularly connected to the PATCO drama, Democratic Representative William Lacy Clay Sr. of Missouri. Clay, an African American from St. Louis, had been active in the Civil Rights Movement and was a founding member of the Congressional Black Caucus. He had served in a city employees union and as education director in Steamfitters Local Number 562 before his election to Congress in 1968. Throughout his congressional career he had held a spot on the House Education and Labor Committee (where he remained until his retirement in 2001).[30] In 1981, Clay was the primary sponsor of H.R. 1576, which would have incorporated PATCO's key demands into law. The sponsor of S. 808, the Senate version of Clay's bill, was Charles McC. Mathias, a liberal Maryland Republican who represented a state with the highest proportion of federal workers in the country.

At the top of the House of Representatives was Speaker Thomas P. "Tip" O'Neill, Democrat of Massachusetts.[31] A lifelong pol, O'Neill had served in the House since 1953, representing a north Boston district vacated by John F. Kennedy when he advanced to the US Senate. A liberal who came out against the Vietnam War in 1967, he had become speaker in 1977 and had already managed the House through turbulent years. Jimmy Carter, a fellow Democrat but Washington outsider, had a strained relationship with Congress; when Massachusetts Senator Edward M. Kennedy challenged Carter in the 1980 Democratic primaries, O'Neill stayed neutral. As he began his third term as speaker, O'Neill faced Ronald Reagan in the White House, a Republican-controlled Senate, and a powerful conservative coalition in the House. He had, by default, become the leading voice in government for regular Democrats. By August 1981, the president's key legislative priorities had passed despite O'Neill's best efforts. When the strike came, he would be caught between his loyalty to the labor movement and his caution about getting caught in the path of the Reagan steamroller. Party leadership carries less weight in the Senate than in the House, but Republican leader Howard

H. Baker Jr. was a moderate Republican from eastern Tennessee who, like the rest of his party in the Senate, was just getting used to serving in a majority. By the time of the strike, however, Baker had shown considerable skill in maneuvering Reagan's tax and spending bills through the minefield of Senate procedures.

The judiciary was also destined to play a role since the day in 1970 when the Federal District Court of the Eastern District of New York imposed a permanent injunction against any future strike by PATCO. The injunction made it possible for the Airline Transportation Association (ATA) to collect large daily damages from PATCO in the event of a future strike. Thus, in 1981, judges such as Thomas C. Platt of Brooklyn and Harold H. Greene of Washington, DC would be in a position to intervene in the strike. Platt was a Nixon appointee; Greene, who fled Nazi Germany with his parents in 1939, was appointed to the federal bench by Jimmy Carter.[32] However, more than a decade had passed since the injunction was imposed, and the question lingered whether courts in 1981 would actually enforce the order.

Among unions, PATCO was only a small part of a much larger American labor movement. It was affiliated with the Maritime Engineers Beneficial Association (MEBA), which itself was a member union in the massive labor umbrella, the American Federation of Labor–Congress of Industrial Organizations (AFL-CIO).

The AFL-CIO would have to make a strategic decision whether to throw its weight behind a PATCO strike. Lane Kirkland led the AFL-CIO, having stepped into the shoes of the legendary George Meany in 1979. Like Jesse Calhoon, head of MEBA, Kirkland served in the Merchant Marine in World War II. While serving, he joined the AFL-affiliated Organization of Masters, Mates, and Pilots. After the war, he received a bachelor's degree from Georgetown University but got a job in the AFL's Research Department. Kirkland's attachment to the AFL went hand in hand with loyalty to the Democratic Party, and he wrote speeches for the party's vice presidential nominee Alben Barkley in 1948 and presidential nominee Adlai Stevenson in 1952 and 1956.[33]

Kirkland's rise to the top of the AFL-CIO began when he joined George Meany's staff as Meany's executive assistant. Meany named him secretary treasurer of the labor behemoth, its number two position, in 1969. Kirkland was a typical liberal of his era—strongly pro-civil rights, pro-welfare state, and anti-Communist. He managed both to be named to Richard M. Nixon's "enemies list" and to lobby successfully against an AFL-CIO endorsement of George McGovern in 1972. Kirkland took on more responsibilities as Meany's health worsened through the 1970s, and when Meany announced his retirement, Kirkland was unanimously elected as the new president. He made it a high priority to bring back into the fold big unions that had bolted from the federation, such as the United Auto Workers and Teamsters. In 1981, he was working to organize labor opposition to Ronald Reagan's conservative domestic agenda and to provide support for the Polish Solidarity labor union.[34]

Other AFL-CIO union leaders made a significant appearance during the PATCO strike, especially Douglas Fraser of the United Auto Workers (still reeling from a Chrysler contract that imposed wage concessions for the first time), William Winpisinger of the Machinists, Ken Blaylock of the American Federation of Government Employees, and Albert Shanker of the American Federation of Teachers. Probably more important to the outcome of the PATCO strike, J. J. O'Donnell was the head of the Air Line Pilots Association. He had been personal friends with previous PATCO president John Leyden and had frequently provided support to PATCO as it attempted to advance its interests. However, O'Donnell had not been pleased with the way Leyden was deposed and was not an admirer of Robert Poli. After stints in the Navy and the Air Force, O'Donnell became a pilot for Eastern Air Lines in 1956. He won local ALPA office two years later and worked his way up the union, serving on the board of directors and the negotiating committee. He became ALPA president in 1971 creating ALPA-PAC (a political action committee for the union) and actively lobbying Congress. He successfully pushed for the first federal anti-hijacking legislation and then, in 1978, for airline deregulation. O'Donnell's political clout led George Meany to give him a seat on the AFL-CIO's executive council, a position typically reserved for members of much larger unions.[35] Like Robert Poli and PATCO, O'Donnell and ALPA endorsed Ronald Reagan in 1980.

Conclusion

Like most significant presidential decisions, Reagan's response to the PATCO strike involved a great many other people in the executive branch, in the coordinate branches, and entirely outside of government. Close presidential advisers including cabinet secretaries, an agency head, directors of the OMB and OPM, policy advisers, a pollster and communications expert, and high-level White House staff played important roles, as did union leaders in and out of PATCO, a founding member of the Black Congressional Caucus, and federal judges in Brooklyn and Washington. That reality is a symbol of both the staggering breadth of the modern federal bureaucracy and the fundamental pluralism of the American political order. The next question is: how did they interact to contribute to the policy result? The crisis would not just be a test of Reagan's leadership. It would be a test of his people and his management style.

CHAPTER 3

Presidential Decision

As PATCO entered 1981, the new leadership of union president Robert E. Poli was determined to prepare for "the definitive strike." This strike would not only gain salary and other concessions but would fundamentally alter PATCO's relationship with the federal government by moving air traffic controllers out of the civil service system and firmly establishing a right to strike. Some observers, like labor economist Herbert R. Northrup, argued that the union actually wanted such a strike and spent 1981 maneuvering to get it.[1] In any event, PATCO leaders expressed a belief that a strike, if it came, could not fail; the controllers were "indispensable" for the continued operation of the air transport system, which itself was essential to the nation's economy.[2]

For his part, Ronald Reagan entered office in January well-disposed to PATCO. In his 1980 campaign, he had indicated to Poli that he would take "whatever steps necessary to provide our air traffic controllers with the most modern equipment available and adjust staff levels and work days so that they are commensurate with achieving a maximum degree of public safety." Poli interpreted Reagan's letter to signal support for new FAA leadership more to PATCO's liking, increased pay, reduced hours, and upgraded equipment. These positions were contained in a "letter of understanding" from the PATCO counsel to the Reagan campaign outlining what PATCO understood Reagan's positions to be.[3]

Reagan received the PATCO endorsement and had proceeded to exempt air traffic controllers from the general federal hiring freeze he instituted by executive memorandum the day he took office. About three weeks later he met with Poli and other labor leaders in the White House, a meeting Poli called "cordial." Reagan also changed the leadership of the FAA, replacing Langhorne Bond with J. Lynn Helms, after giving the union the opportunity to object to Helms and apparently receiving no complaint. At the Department of Transportation, which oversees the FAA, Reagan appointed Drew Lewis, who expressed sympathy for the controllers in his confirmation hearings (while also warning against an illegal strike).[4] The Reagan team's strategy, extending from the 1980 campaign into his presidency, was to split off a portion of the labor union movement and attach "patriotic and socially conservative" union members to a new Republican coalition. This meant, among other things, treating Reagan's few labor friends well and not provoking unnecessary confrontations with the labor movement.[5]

In Congress, Representative William Lacy Clay Sr. (D-MO) introduced H.R. 1576 in early 1981. The bill, which was written with assistance from PATCO, would have met PATCO's key demands, including their proposed pay increase and revision of the 1978 Civil Service Reform Act to allow strikes by the union. While some PATCO members were encouraged by Clay's bill, others were skeptical. Their skepticism was warranted. The expense of the legislation, as well as its removal of barriers to strikes, made it a tough sell in an increasingly conservative Congress. While the administration expressed a desire to come to terms with the controllers, it also opposed H.R. 1576, deeming its estimated five-year price tag of $13 billion as extravagant, and David Stockman's Office of Management and Budget testified against it in House hearings.[6]

The Crisis Arrives

For months after Reagan's inauguration, the matter of the air traffic controllers was handled by Secretary of Transportation Drew Lewis, FAA head J. Lynn Helms, and the negotiating team Lewis chose to represent the government in its dealings with PATCO. The law firm of Morgan, Lewis, and Bockius, which had acquired a reputation as tough on labor, was selected for this role in February 1981.[7] PATCO pushed its proposal for a $10,000 raise, a thirty-two (rather than forty) hour work week, and a better retirement package.

As the negotiations began, the administration assumed that PATCO's fall 1980 demands were a highball opening bid. The Office of Management and Budget, cognizant of the long-term fiscal implications and calling the controllers "overpaid" and "pampered," argued for a tough line in the negotiations. In keeping with federal law, the FAA called pay and hours nonnegotiable, but the White House did not set any bottom line in advance. At the first negotiating session on February 12, according to mediators from the Federal Mediation and Conciliation Service, PATCO reps aggressively threatened a strike.[8]

On April 28, Robert Poli broke off negotiations with the FAA, citing insufficient progress after thirty-seven meetings. Two days later, Poli testified before the House Committee on Post Office and Civil Service and denied that PATCO intended to strike—a denial he repeated in other venues—while also implicitly threatening one, and the union accelerated its strike preparations.[9]

On May 22, Poli's appearance of ambivalence was abandoned. He told a PATCO convention that if the FAA "did not come to their senses, I vow to you that the skies will be silent. . . . The only illegal strike is an unsuccessful strike."[10] The PATCO board announced at the convention, to raucous cheers, that it had set June 22 as a possible strike date.

As early as February 1981, an internal administration analysis warned about a possible PATCO strike or "work to rule" slowdown. Calling PATCO "one of the most, if not the most, aggressive of all federal unions," the document cited a Heritage Foundation analysis calling for a "tough stance" including criminal charges and sanctions against strikers.[11] Even before negotiations opened, Drew Lewis and J. Lynn Helms began upgrading the FAA contingency plan for keeping air traffic flowing in the event of a strike. In May, the White House had asked for a copy of the FAA strike plan.[12] Lewis and Helms revised Langhorne Bond's plan, making it more robust and capable of handling a more severe interruption.

Poli's May 22 strike threat drew the attention of the White House. Secretary of the Cabinet Craig Fuller began monitoring the talks closely, informing Presidential Counselor Ed Meese of developments. Drew Lewis asked for additional negotiating flexibility, especially regarding pay. The OMB strongly opposed Lewis's request and proposed a 5 percent salary add-on instead.[13] At a June 11 meeting Lewis unveiled his proposal, which included: a 10 percent pay raise for controllers who doubled as trainers; a 20 percent (rather than 10 percent) pay differential for nighttime shifts; a thirty-seven-and-a-half-hour week accomplished by giving a daily thirty-minute paid lunch break; a guarantee of no more than six and a half hours per day at an operating position; one year of severance pay for anyone with five or more years of service if disqualified for medical reasons; and investment in new equipment. The union was also offered a formal consultative role in FAA decision-making.[14] The estimated total cost of the package was $40 million over the previous contract.

Perhaps surprisingly, given that negotiation hardliners including Meese and OMB Director David Stockman were present, the group approved Lewis's proposal. The next day, word came down that Reagan had given his final approval as well—his first major decision in this episode. As Joseph A. McCartin points out, "Never before had the government offered so much in negotiation with a federal employee union."[15] Most notably, Lewis's proposal burst through the restriction on hours and wages bargaining. A contract reached on this basis would require congressional action to revise the law.

Lewis personally joined the next round of contract talks in order to present his (now the administration's) proposal. However, Poli was disdainful. The government's concessions seem to have convinced the PATCO leadership that it had the administration on the run and should press its advantage. On June 18, Craig Fuller reported to Reagan and the "Troika"—Meese, Chief of Staff James Baker, and Deputy Chief of Staff Michael Deaver—that a strike was likely and that more might need to be given on pay and hours. Lewis wanted authorization to make additional concessions, a stance that was fought by Donald Devine, head of the Office of Personnel Management. Devine was concerned not only about PATCO but the possible repercussions for other federal employee unions, especially the postal workers, who were also in contract negotiations and had set a tentative strike date in early August. If PATCO had been the most militant federal union over the last decade or more, the postal workers would rate a close second. When wildcat strikes by two hundred thousand postal workers erupted in 1970, Richard Nixon had sent the National Guard to New York City to try to deliver mail. When that failed miserably, the government capitulated.[16] Ever since, the postal unions had jostled for the upper hand. Devine argued that it was time to stop fueling this runaway train of federal employees unions, and he won the day. In the end, no new concessions for PATCO were approved. Instead, at a June 20 meeting, the contingency plan was discussed, and a decision was made to alert the Justice Department to the possibility that a strike might lead to arrests and prosecutions.[17]

Another factor also suddenly militated against further concessions from the administration. While Reagan's October 1980 letter to Poli was already in circulation, the letter from PATCO General Counsel Richard Leighton to the Reagan campaign specifying the conditions for a PATCO endorsement became public only days before the June 22 strike deadline.[18] The exchange of letters was investigated by the House Committee on Public Works and Transportation at the insistence of some House Democrats who considered it indicative of an improper deal between Reagan and the union. Leighton denied that the letters were evidence of a deal. Though the investigation concluded there was "no evidence" of a quid pro quo or any violation of federal election law, suspicions were in the air, and it instantly became more difficult for Reagan to bend any further.[19]

As the hourglass was running out on the deadline, Poli's approach suddenly shifted from defiance to accommodation. During a break in the negotiations the night of June 21, the union president had gotten word that "horse counts" supporting a strike were below the threshold the union had set, 80 percent of all controllers. The union leadership had long seen a successful strike vote as crucial to maximizing their contract gains. The failure of the vote was now known by Poli and deduced by the government when the union did not announce a 7 a.m. strike as planned. Poli returned to the table in a much more agreeable state of mind. Shortly before the deadline struck, Poli agreed to a tentative proposal largely based on Lewis's framework. Of ninety-six contract points reached in the 1978 agreement, the new agreement retained ninety-two without change. At the end, Poli's loss of fighting spirit was evident to the FAA negotiators, whose efforts to withdraw previously offered government concessions were only limited by Drew Lewis.[20] The proposed contract provided each controller with a $4,000 raise (above what Congress had decreed for all federal employees); time and a half for more than thirty-six hours a week; fourteen weeks' severance pay in case of medical disqualification; a 15 percent night differential; and some other minor concessions.[21]

Outsiders tended to see the contract as a win for PATCO, a view shared by PATCO ally Jesse Calhoon of MEBA, PATCO nemesis Langhorne Bond, and labor critics in the National Right to Work movement. Former PATCO lobbyist Joseph S. Miller believed that "Drew Lewis was bending over backwards in negotiations to satisfy as many of PATCO's demands as he could" and that "Lewis felt obligated to go the extra mile."[22] Lewis geared up to defend the contract against conservatives in Congress, spending July defending the $40 million bump as the administration's bottom line and emphasizing the importance of fiscal responsibility.[23] However, it was PATCO itself that wound up turning against the agreement.

When Poli signed on to the agreement, he declared it "fair" and promised to fight for its endorsement by the union. Supporters within the union pointed to four reasons the agreement should be ratified: the FAA had actually agreed to negotiate over pay for the first time; a precedent was set that could ultimately lead controllers out of the civil service; funds were assured for retraining and other goals high on PATCO's list (though not at the top); and supporters in Congress had confidently promised to push enabling legislation through at an early date.[24] However, the Choirboys, the militants who had been preparing for a strike for years, were not supportive. The agreement, they felt, had fallen too far short of PATCO's original demands. They also wondered what more the union might have gotten had there been a favorable strike vote on June 22. The PATCO board quickly recommended rejection of the proposed contract; even Poli voted "no." Ultimately, the membership voted overwhelmingly against it—616 yes to 13,495 no.[25] The union came back to (and embellished) its original demands, which the administration had considered flatly unacceptable from the beginning: a $10,000 a year raise, a thirty-two-hour work week, and a much more generous retirement package. The administration estimated PATCO's package would cost $681 million a year, a figure seventeen times greater than it had offered. Facing an administration unwilling to move any farther in its direction, PATCO called a strike beginning at 7 a.m. on August 3. There remains controversy over whether the vote approving the strike actually reached the 80 percent mark this time, either. The "validation agents" double-checking the votes were drawn from the Choirboys, and given what was known about the vote in some major air traffic centers, some observers questioned their totals. Others, including Jack Maher, alleged that the three-tiered voting system built into strike planning had been diluted to ensure a positive vote to strike.[26]

The question remains today whether Poli lost control of his union or whether he himself had orchestrated the scene, agreeing to terms on the surface but maneuvering behind the scenes to goad a rejection from his board. Former PATCO president John F. Leyden, who supported the contract and was recruited by Poli to help sell it to the members, argued the former, saying that "disproportionate democracy led to a runaway ship."[27] Perhaps strike agitation had so infused the membership that momentum for a strike was out of control. Others argued the latter, pointing out that Poli had always dominated his board and that the outcome—a strike—was exactly what Poli himself had predicted and prepared for over the previous year. Perhaps he had executed a tactical "good cop, bad cop" maneuver. Labor economist Herbert R. Northrup has argued strongly for this proposition, relying not only on deductive reasoning but on internal PATCO documents and interviews with PATCO leaders.[28] Whatever the intentions behind Poli's machinations, even sympathetic observers feared that PATCO was heading for a crash.

Throughout the negotiations, the administration sent many signals, both implicit and explicit, that a strike would not be tolerated. On April 30, Lewis said that recognition of the contributions of air traffic controllers would continue but "within the accepted framework of federal employment"—a not-too-subtle reference to the no-strike provision in federal law. After the PATCO board issued its June 22 strike deadline, the FAA instructed supervisors to remind their controllers about their legal obligations, then sent personal letters from FAA Director Helms to controllers' homes. On June 17, in the midst of the first strike scare, Lewis said more plainly that "a strike would constitute an illegal action, with PATCO and individual controllers subject to criminal prosecution." On June 21, Reagan instructed Lewis to tell Poli he was the best friend PATCO had ever had in the White House but "would not countenance an illegal strike nor would I permit negotiations while such a strike was in process." On July 31, as the strike loomed, the secretary of transportation condemned PATCO for having "set a strike deadline in blatant disregard for the fact that a strike would be illegal."[29] Despite these warnings, "PATCO did not reckon with Reagan stepping outside what the union took as the 'rules'"[30]—that is, the precedent of accommodation set by previous administrations.

If the multiple statements from the administration warning against an illegal strike were not enough, PATCO might have noticed worrisome signs of congressional opinion, as well. House transportation subcommittee chairman Norman Mineta wrote to Poli on June 1 asking clarification about PATCO's reported intention to strike, mentioning pointedly that Poli had told Mineta's subcommittee more than once that there would be "no strike."[31] Shortly thereafter, Poli was lectured in congressional testimony by one congressman, who told Poli: "We have very little sympathy for [a strike]. The FAA has said they are going to be firm, maybe even more than firm. The Justice Department has said they are going to be firm. . . . There is only one thing that is going to come about as a result of the walkout. You and your people are going to lose. You are just going to lose."[32]

In hearings, Congressman Barry M. Goldwater Jr. likewise complained that PATCO was asking for pay that was "substantially more than a Cabinet member . . . or the Commanding General of the Air Force."[33]

In the immediate wake of the June 22 strike scare, the union's biggest congressional supporter, William Clay, reintroduced his bill, which had gone nowhere, shorn of the top two pay grades and the implied right to strike.[34] Then, on the eve of the strike, fifty-five senators and nineteen representatives sent a letter to PATCO describing the most recent FAA offer as fair, reminding the union of the no-strike provisions of federal law, warning that Congress would not be receptive to a strike, and calling on the administration to deal with any strike with "the full force of the law."[35]

It did not matter. The union rejected the government's request for seven additional days for negotiation. PATCO's demands remained several hundred million dollars above the administration's $40 million "bottom line," and the union gave the government three days to negotiate a solution. On July 31, Lewis met with Meese, Fuller, and others to consider last-ditch options. Lewis felt blindsided by Poli, and a number of fiscal and political considerations worked against moving any farther in PATCO's direction, including fears that additional concessions would be a dangerous sign of weakness to other federal unions and even foreign powers.[36] It was not the first or last time the international implications were a major consideration. The group did agree to Lewis's idea of proposing that the government offer PATCO the same amount ($40 million) that the failed contract would have cost in the same period, but with a lengthened timeframe that brought the overall total to $50 million and with flexibility to allocate the amount as the union chose. The night before the strike deadline, Lewis informed Poli that Reagan had given him three instructions: "To conduct no negotiations during a strike, to fire those who struck, and to offer no amnesty to those fired."[37]

When PATCO dismissed the offer and the warning, the strike proceeded—at the start of the busiest travel month of the year. The contingency plan, which was further rewritten and bolstered by the FAA with cooperation from the airlines after the June 22 strike scare, was immediately put into effect. Supervisors and military controllers filled in, private air traffic was temporarily halted, airlines prioritized their routes, and the FAA utilized a new centralized "flow control" system that rationalized the schedule nationwide.[38] On the first day of the strike, about seven thousand flights were cancelled, but at least 50 percent of normal air traffic was maintained; within a few weeks, the system was handling an estimated 80 percent of normal traffic.[39]

Presidential Considerations

At this point, the president had to decide what course of action to take. Reagan had a range of options.

In theory, he could agree to give the union what it wanted (although many of PATCO's demands would need to be approved by Congress, too). This option was not seriously considered.

He could allow the strike to proceed, make the most of the contingency plan, and hope to return to the negotiating table.

The dispute could be taken to binding arbitration.

Or Reagan could take a tougher line, adopting one or more of the following policies: requesting that courts fine PATCO for violating the 1970 injunction; seeking to decertify the union, stripping it of its position as the recognized bargaining agent for air traffic controllers; firing the strikers; and/or prosecuting some or all of the strikers.

A number of considerations came into play, and taking a tough stand against PATCO carried a variety of serious risks. As the strike began, there was no way to know with certainty how well the contingency plan, which was still being revised the weekend before the strike, would work, or for how long it could be sustained. After all, no one ever knows how good a contingency plan is until it needs to be implemented.

There was an economic risk involved, even if the contingency plan worked relatively well. Some internal administration estimates held that a strike would create "economic havoc" costing the economy between $62 million and $150 million a day for as long as the strike lasted.[40] Beyond the general damage, particular concerns were raised about the health of the aviation industry. This, as the nation was already sliding toward the second half of a double-dip recession.

Finally, and certainly not least, was the danger that air safety might be compromised. An airline crash attributable to the strike would not only be an enormous human tragedy but could easily turn public opinion heavily against Reagan. As Dinesh D'Souza argued, "If there had been an accident, the political consequences for Reagan might have been catastrophic."[41] This was a danger the controllers themselves played up with talk of "aluminum rain" and "planes falling from the sky."

On the other hand, several considerations justified a tougher line.[42] For one thing, the economic consequences cut both ways. It was clear that a prolonged strike would hurt an economy that was already in serious trouble. While that fact could provide an argument for reaching a deal, it could just as easily point to a policy of breaking the strike quickly.

Furthermore, the government was then engaged in contract talks with Treasury Department workers who were unionized and the postal workers were in the midst of voting on their proposed contract. After coming to terms with government negotiators in light of the government's hard line with PATCO after June 22, the postal workers voted overwhelmingly to approve their contract. The administration was very cognizant of not giving the impression that it was following a "strike avoidance policy" that might invite further labor unrest and even more exorbitant demands.

PATCO's demands were also clearly at variance with Reagan's budget aims. He was being asked to bust the federal budget while in the midst of a hard fight to win approval from Congress for his budget discipline measures. To do so could significantly undermine his policy accomplishment both symbolically and substantively.

The PATCO endorsement of Reagan in 1980 may have actually worked against the union, since the administration already risked the appearance of favoritism with its seemingly generous (but rejected) proposal. That risk was heightened with the recent publication of the Leighton letter. To go even farther in PATCO's direction would stimulate further questions about whether Reagan was "paying off" the union for its 1980 support.

After having issued numerous warnings against a strike through spokesmen, if Reagan tolerated the strike when the gauntlet was laid down, he would also foster an obvious appearance of weakness. That appearance of weakness would hurt him not just in future union negotiations, but in his dealings with Congress and even foreign leaders.

Drew Lewis later argued that the PATCO strike carried national security implications having to do with control of US airspace. Lewis held that PATCO "had to know" about the national security problems caused by a strike: "We knew they were savvy and knew of the implications."[43] This by itself made the strike unacceptable.

For Reagan, however, the decisive issue was the simple fact that PATCO strikers had violated the law and their personal oaths. In previous meetings on the subject, former White House counselor Edwin Meese said Reagan had been "absolutely firm" about enforcing the law.[44] Even in the privacy of his diary, Reagan was consistent on this point. In his PATCO-related entry on June 21, Reagan emphasized the illegality of the strike; on August 1–2, after noting he learned a strike was imminent, he wrote "That's against the law"; on August 5, after remarking that Lane Kirkland joined the PATCO picket line, he asked "How do they explain approving of law-breaking—to say nothing of violation of an oath taken by each a.c. that he or she would not strike."[45] No other justification for the firing is found in Reagan's diary.

PATCO and the Law

At this point, it is important to examine in some detail the basis for Reagan's view that the strikers were lawbreakers. First, federal statutory law prohibited federal employees from striking. Second, the controllers were required to take an oath of employment in which they pledged not to strike. Finally, starting in 1970, the union faced a permanent federal court order that enjoined it from striking.

At the time of the strike, the prohibition on strikes by federal employees was found in three statutes. The first barred from federal employment "any person who participates in a strike, asserts the right to strike against the government, or is a member of a government employees organization that asserts that right." (It also bars employment of anyone advocating the overthrow of the government, thus placing strikers on the same level as revolutionaries.) The second statute made violations of the first a felony punishable by up to one year in prison and a $1,000 fine. The third made striking against the government an unfair labor practice. It was also illegal to aid or abet those violating the anti-strike statutes.[46] The history of the statutory prohibition reached back to 1946, though as recently as the 1978 Civil Service Reform Act it had been reaffirmed and strengthened by mandating that the Federal Labor Relations Authority decertify labor organizations that violate the no-strike provisions. In 1971, the Supreme Court had upheld the constitutionality of the no-strike law when it affirmed without comment the lower court decision in *United Federation of Postal Clerks v. Blount*.

The statutes undergirded the oath of employment. Every air traffic controller, and every other member of the federal civilian employment, was required to swear in writing the following oath: "I am not participating in any strike against the Government of the United States or any agency thereof, and I will not participate while an employee of the Government of the United States or any agency thereof."[47]

The injunction was granted in 1970 at the request of the Air Transport Association (ATA), the organization representing the nation's airlines, which argued that a controllers strike would be highly damaging to the aviation industry. However, the injunction had never been enforced by the government against subsequent PATCO "job actions."

The President's Decision

In the end, Reagan chose the toughest response available to him: the administration sought and received major fines against PATCO sequestered from the union's strike fund—fines that ultimately exceeded $1 million a day. By late November the union faced $150 million in outstanding fines and other penalties, including $28.9 million awarded by courts to the Air Transport Association for violation of the 1970 injunction.[48] The administration also immediately began the process of decertifying the union, both as a punitive action and, perhaps, some suggested, as a measure that might give Poli a face-saving way out (as he could then use the argument that "rather than end the union, we better go back to work").[49] Most dramatically, Reagan fired the strikers, and the Justice Department prosecuted the strike leaders. For months, Reagan had made clear his intended policy—in the event of a strike, there would be no concessions, no negotiations, and no amnesty. This was his second, and most dramatic, decision of the saga.

With the strike only a few hours old, Reagan confirmed a decision in a key meeting with Meese, Attorney General William French Smith, White House Communications Director David Gergen, and others to give the strikers forty-eight hours to return to their jobs or be fired. The PATCO situation had heretofore been handled for the most part by Lewis and Helms. The two supported a strong response, though Lewis had also prevailed on Reagan to hold the ultimatum until the strike began and the contingency plan was operating.[50] There is no question, though, that Reagan made the final call. The decision-making process was consistent with his overall management style, in which he delegated details to subordinates along with general guidance in the form of a firm philosophical direction. In this case the general guidance consisted of sympathy for the controllers' grievances combined with a strong commitment to budget control and an even stronger aversion to illegal strikes. Lewis affirmed later that Reagan had been kept thoroughly informed of developments in the negotiations.[51] When a final decision had to be made, it was forwarded to Reagan. As Laurence I. Barrett argued, his risky decision, "like others he took, came directly from Reagan's gut."[52] Donald Devine later agreed that "The decision to dismiss the striking controllers was a personal decision of the president." Devine even contended that "Most of his major advisors on the matter opposed his decision to issue an ultimatum."[53] This assertion is questionable—it is clear, for example, that Lewis and Helms agreed with Reagan—but there is no question that Reagan ultimately weighed the risks and made the decision.

On the same lines, former White House Counsel Peter J. Wallison contends that "Most politicians, confronted with this crisis and mindful of the potential consequences of an air disaster, would have sought a face-saving solution—a commission, a White House meeting followed by a compromise, or submitting conciliatory legislation to Congress. . . . Not Reagan."[54]

In the August 3 meeting, Reagan was briefed on the implementation of the contingency plan and on the Justice Department's plans for seeking an injunction and filing criminal complaints. Reagan himself declared, "Dammit, the law is the law and the law says they cannot strike. . . . Suspension, hell. If the law says they can't strike, and if they then go on strike, then they've quit. Period." According to David Gergen's notes, Reagan was "very animated" at this point in the discussion. Reagan also made a distinction in the meeting between private and public employment and expressed the belief that he had little choice in the matter. "They have terminated—They're in defiance of the law." Though advised by Smith that he could lawfully fire the controllers immediately, Reagan contended that "In order for this message to reach everyone, [we] need 48 hours. I'm willing to say 48 hours."[55]

Deputy Chief of Staff Michael Deaver would later relate in an oral history interview:

I don't think he thought of it as a seminal moment, but it turned out to be. It was interesting to me, because it goes right to this business about staff, and who's making the decisions. I remember that morning in the Cabinet meeting—the Cabinet's all around the table, and everybody had ideas, and Drew Lewis—who was [Secretary of] Transportation—and others were going back and forth across the table. I looked over at Reagan, because it dawned on me that he wasn't saying anything. He was writing on his yellow pad, writing, writing, writing. This went on for about 15 minutes, and finally I heard him say, "Excuse me, fellows, but let me just read you something here. Tell me what you think about it." It was the statement he gave in the Rose Garden about half an hour later, word for word. Nobody changed anything. Everybody said, "Oh, yes, that's great."

But it wasn't a surprise to me, because it had been a Reagan position in California when the firefighters, I think it was, went out. Reagan said, "A public employee does not have the right to strike. How can you strike against the public? They're the people who hire you." He'd had that experience with teachers, saying, "They insist on the right to strike and tenure at the same time, how can you do this?" So it wasn't a real surprise to me. I guess what was the surprise was that in this first example of his own action, it was pure Reagan, and it wasn't changed in any way.[56]

Domestic policy advisor Martin Anderson would later observe:

What he did with PATCO—at the time it was presented, they were going to strike. When he was told about it, he just said, "No, they can't strike." It looked like off the top of his head he had done that. Well, when we were putting together this book *Reagan, In His Own Hand*, my wife and I found some of these essays that he had written dealing with strikes by public employees. Many years ago he had very carefully laid out, analyzed it, studied it, and said, "Look, they cannot strike. And if they strike, they're gone."

So what we did not realize while we were in the White House with him was that he had already thought about this. He had worked out the theory, he had a whole thing all set up. Then they came and said they're striking and he said, "Fine, they're gone."[57]

Peter Wallison, White House Counsel for Reagan at the time, agrees with Anderson. Reagan, Wallison notes, "had long before articulated the views that would shape his response, and he stood by them."[58]

After the meeting, Reagan appeared and spoke to the nation. His public statement reiterated and amplified his private comments. The union demands, Reagan pointed out, added up to $681 million, seventeen times what PATCO's president had agreed to in June. "This would impose a tax burden on their fellow citizens which is unacceptable." He went on, renewing his argument about the difference between the private and public sectors: "Government cannot close down the assembly line. It has to provide without interruption the protective services which are the government's reason for being. It was in recognition of this fact that the Congress passed a law forbidding strikes by government employees against the public safety." He then read verbatim the non-strike oath taken by controllers and delivered the ultimatum: "It is for this reason that I must tell those who fail to report for duty this morning that they are in violation of the law, and if they do not report for work within forty-eight hours, they have forfeited their jobs and will be terminated." When pressed by reporters as to why he did not take a lesser action first, Reagan replied, "What lesser action can there be? The law is very explicit. They are violating the law."[59] Drew Lewis, by Reagan's side, added that strikers "will not be government employees at any time in the future."

Some scholars have argued that Reagan was not legally obligated to take such action immediately. In this view, firing the strikers was evidence of a lack of "good faith" bargaining, a violation of federal labor law.[60] In Reagan's view, the administration's June offer was the best that could be done, and the union had left no room for further discussion with its illegal conduct and its ballooning demands. An August 25 report issued by the Federal Labor Relations Authority rejected PATCO's claim that the administration had engaged in unfair labor practices, finding instead that the union had done so by allowing only three days of additional negotiations after rejection of the June 22 contract.[61] Many PATCO members expressed a feeling of betrayal by Reagan, after having endorsed him and receiving from him the sympathetic letter of October 20, 1980. A reading of the letter, however, shows that Reagan discussed equipment modernization, staff levels, and workdays, but not pay, and certainly not encouragement or permission for a strike. Some PATCO supporters have even argued that the administration wanted a strike so that an example could be made. This seems unlikely. There is no supporting evidence in the documentary record, and it cannot explain why the administration made such a generous offer in June or why Reagan gave the union a forty-eight-hour window to return to work.[62]

An extensive legal analysis by Bernard D. Meltzer and Cass R. Sunstein shows that Reagan had good reason to believe he was obligated to fire the strikers. The primary statute in question said that a person "may not accept or hold a position in the Government of the United States" if he "participates in a strike . . . against the Government of the United States"—a declaration, Meltzer and Sunstein note, "of his ineligibility binding in general on the executive." After reviewing the development of the anti-strike provisions, the authors conclude that "The statutory language is unambiguous, and its history tends to suggest that the words were intended to mean what they said"—lenient practice by previous administrations notwithstanding. Some opportunity for executive discretion remained to Reagan, and he used it. He may have been legally required to fire the strikers, but he had some authority to define who the strikers were. Hence the forty-eight-hour deadline—those who returned in time were not considered to have participated in the strike.[63]

Of the nation's air traffic controllers, nearly 13,000 struck on August 3. About 3,400 did not go on strike, approximately 1,300 struck but returned, and the remaining 11,345 (or thereabouts) struck, stayed off the job, and were fired when the forty-eight-hour deadline expired.[64] On August 5, in keeping with the president's deadline, Drew Lewis declared that the strike was "over with" and began sending out dismissal notices to the remaining strikers.

In accordance with the FAA's strike contingency plan, 3,291 supervisors were pressed into service, along with about 800 military controllers and 1,000 newly hired personnel. Within a month of the firings, nearly 1,500 furloughed airline pilots were also hired as controllers. Short-staffed centers meant many controllers around the country were working sixty hours a week. Within a month, the FAA received 125,000 applications for open controller positions. Training of new controllers at the FAA's Oklahoma City facility ramped up, as three hundred retired controllers were hired as additional trainers.[65]

Just as Reagan had largely allowed his appointees—particularly Drew Lewis and J. Lynn Helms—to manage the situation until the point of decision, he also delegated to Lewis and others the task of implementing the decision. *Newsweek* reported that the White House felt Lewis handled the crisis "nearly flawlessly."[66] Reagan's reliance on delegation misfired badly in the Iran-Contra episode, but author Laurence I. Barrett judges that, in the PATCO instance, it worked well: "Reagan had an unusually competent Transportation Secretary in Drew Lewis, a man who could handle the aftermath of the air traffic controllers' strike without constant heckling from the Oval Office."[67]

In his autobiography *An American Life*, published a decade after the PATCO strike, Reagan himself recounted that on Sunday, August 2, Drew Lewis informed him that PATCO was threatening to strike the following day "because of our refusal to meet its demand for a huge salary increase."

> Although I had accepted the argument that the unusual pressures and demands in their occupation justified an increase, their demands would have cost taxpayers almost $700 million a year. I told Lewis to advise the union's leaders that, as a former union president, I was probably the best friend his organization ever had in the White House, but I could not countenance an illegal strike nor permit negotiations to take place as long as one was in progress. I hoped the air controllers realized I meant what I said. . . .
>
> Unions can strike a private business and shut it down, but you cannot allow a strike to shut down a vital government service.
>
> Governments are different from private industry. I agreed with Calvin Coolidge, who said "There is no right to strike against the public safety by anyone, anywhere, at any time."
>
> Congress had passed a law forbidding strikes by government employees, and every member of the controllers' union had signed a sworn affidavit agreeing not to strike. I told Lewis to tell leaders of the union that I expected them to abide by it. . . .
>
> I suppose this was the first real national emergency I faced as

president. The strike endangered the safety of thousands of passengers on hundreds of airline flights daily, and threatened more harm to our already troubled economy. But I never had any doubt how to respond to it. . . .

Citing the pledge made by controllers never to strike, I said that if they did not return to work within forty-eight hours, their jobs would be terminated. I didn't like disrupting the lives and careers of these professionals, many of whom had spent years serving their country. I don't like firing anybody. But I realized that if they made the decision not to return to work in the full knowledge of what I'd said, then I wasn't firing them, they were giving up their jobs based on their individual decisions.[68]

Reagan adhered steadfastly to his hard line, despite considerable pressures to relent. On August 5, the day the deadline arrived, he expressed sympathy for the strikers: "I am sorry for them. I think that these are fine people out there who have been misled and who don't quite understand that our position has to be irreversible. There is a law and an oath that they signed. . . . I certainly take no joy out of this. And I was hoping that more of them would recognize the obligation they have. But there is just no other choice."[69] A flurry of proposals bubbled up, sent by innovators to Martin Anderson in an attempt to resolve the crisis short of mass firings. Some within the administration proposed privatizing the system, others proposed phasing in the firings at one thousand a day, starting with most senior strikers. Most of these proposals emerged after the firings were announced on August 5, too late to avoid the appearance of ignominious retreat by the president.[70]

Lane Kirkland, as head of the AFL-CIO, privately made it known through an intermediary that he would be willing to help the administration stop the strike. Kirkland's plan had three parts: Poli and other PATCO leaders would resign, admit the strike was illegal, and admit that they had misled the union's rank and file. Reagan would rehire the rest of the strikers. And Kirkland himself would issue a statement declaring that the strike was illegal and that the president had acted properly.[71] The plan would have solved many of Reagan's problems, but not the one that vexed him most—his determination to hold firm against the illegality of the strike by depriving illegal strikers of their positions. In any event, PATCO leaders dismissed Kirkland's proposal.[72]

Ken Blaylock, president of the American Federation of Government Employees, then approached Donald Devine at OPM. Devine was a strong conservative who favored the president's decision to fire the strikers but also feared the expense of training a new complement of controllers. Devine told Blaylock there could be no negotiations while an illegal strike was ongoing. Blaylock proposed the expedient of having Poli order the strikers back to work for ten days, during which public negotiations would "reach" an agreement that had already been secretly ironed out in advance. Even before the administration had a chance to reject this Rube Goldberg scheme, PATCO leadership caught wind of it and preemptively dismissed it, too.[73]

If entreaties from labor to revise his position were substantial, Reagan also faced pressures from a very different direction. According to Drew Lewis, some of Reagan's wealthy California friends who owned private jets were so irritated by the inconvenience of the strike that they threatened to try to have Lewis fired. When Lewis told Reagan of these machinations, the president's response was, "You let me worry about my friends, you worry about the strike."[74]

In an August 13 press conference at his California ranch, Reagan said "There is no strike.... What they did was terminate their own employment by quitting.... I just don't see any way that it could be expected that we could now just go back and pretend they weren't breaking the law or breaking their oath." In that press conference, the president also noted that flights were at 80 percent of normal and that more than a hundred thousand people had travelled on transatlantic flights the day before, expressing that "Our obligation is to those several thousand that are in there working. And I must say they have my utmost gratitude and admiration and I think they should have of all the people for what they're doing."[75] The next day, Congressman William D. Ford (D-MI) wrote to Reagan calling for the president to establish a blue-ribbon panel to survey the impasse and recommend a solution. He responded by scrawling "no way" in the margins.[76]

The coup de grâce was administered to any sort of backchannel negotiations when Labor Secretary Raymond Donovan told an audience in Mississippi on August 21 that the administration was looking for a way out of the impasse. The White House immediately disowned Donovan's statement, Lewis reaffirmed publicly that strikers would not be rehired, and Ed Meese told Devine and others that all discussion of rehiring, public or private, must cease. On September 3, Reagan arrived at the one hundredth anniversary convention of the United Brotherhood of Carpenters, where he had been invited to speak months before. His advisers had given him a draft speech that carefully avoided mention of the PATCO controversy. Instead, Reagan put an exclamation point on his policy, telling his union audience that "We cannot, as citizens, pick and choose the laws we will or will not obey.... You are the employers of all who serve in government, elected or appointed, and none of us in government can strike against you and the interests of you, the sovereign people."[77] According to reports, the carpenters received his message politely.

Rehiring, Prosecution, and Decertification

Aside from firing the strikers, Reagan approved two additional immediate steps against PATCO. First, seventy-eight union leaders were prosecuted—individuals the Justice Department called "a small number of the most culpable strike leaders."[78] The department justified this selective prosecution by the expectation that prosecutions at the top of the organization would "maximize the deterrent value of prosecution and facilitate the gathering of proof."[79] After the first few days of the strike, when half a dozen union leaders (including vice president Gary Eads) were jailed, a decision was made in the Justice Department to pursue fines rather than incarceration in most cases.

Second, the administration, acting under provisions of the Civil Service Reform Act of 1978, sought to have the strike declared an "unfair labor practice" resulting in the decertification of PATCO as the exclusive organizational representative of air traffic controllers. This outcome would essentially serve as a death sentence for the union, which would no longer have standing to collect funds through dues checkoff or to negotiate with the federal government on behalf of its members. On October 22, the Federal Labor Relations Authority (FLRA) voted 2–1 to adopt the recommendation of the FAA that PATCO be decertified immediately. All three members agreed that the union had committed an unfair labor practice as defined by law; the difference of opinion was over the remedy. The decertification order declared that "PATCO was open and flagrant in its violation, demonstrating a willful defiance of law as well as court mandate in a situation wherein the strike critically impacted on the public interest."[80] Lewis praised the decision, arguing that it "affirms a basic principle of our democracy, that no person or organization is above the law and that the citizens of this country cannot be allowed to pick and choose the laws they will obey."[81] The decision became effective on November 3, exactly three months after the beginning of the strike.

Reagan's decision to fire the controllers was not a single decision made at one point in time, but it was a choice that unfolded over several years as Reagan deliberately refused to reverse himself. If PATCO's unwillingness to deal was an obstacle to rehiring, an even bigger one according to labor intermediaries was Reagan's own adamant opposition.[82] Indeed, not only did Reagan refuse to rehire the strikers to their old positions, the controllers were banned from employment by private contractors working for the FAA or interfacing with the Defense Department; they were shut out of employment by the post office until Congressman Ford intervened in 1982; and the State Department worked to prevent their employment by foreign countries. Fired controllers were also required to refund the government for moving expenses paid to them to relocate to a new facility within one year of the strike's beginning.[83] As months passed, the president came under growing pressure from the labor movement, the media, and some in Congress to rehire the fired controllers. As the reasoning went, Reagan had won, the union was destroyed, and leniency could now be afforded. Having argued that Reagan was legally obligated to fire the strikers, Meltzer and Sunstein contend that he did possess considerable discretion to rehire them. The key 1955 statute bars employment of one who "participates"—present tense—in a strike, and the Taft-Hartley Act which served as a basis for the 1955 act established a three-year (not permanent) ban on employment.[84]

However, for Reagan, any mass rehiring would undercut the impact of the firing. If illegal strikers got their old jobs back, the firing would not have made much difference. There were additional arguments against rehiring, not least of which were potential negative effects on the morale of those controllers who had stayed on the job and the likelihood of tensions between the courageous strikers (or scofflaws) and the loyal controllers (or scabs), as the two groups would interact. Since safe operations require harmonious coordination between controllers in a facility, this potential for disharmony could have very serious consequences. (A survey of continuing controllers showed a large majority unconditionally opposed to rehiring fired strikers.[85]) A selective, as opposed to mass, rehiring could subject the FAA to charges of discriminatory hiring.

The pressure to rehire the controllers came to a crescendo in December, four months after the firings. On December 1, Reagan intimated that he might be open to allowing striking controllers to apply for other positions in the federal government, though not their old jobs. He tentatively repeated that suggestion in a meeting the next day with the AFL-CIO executive council at the White House, though he did not commit to it. The focus of the meeting was PATCO, with the union leaders turning up the heat in an attempt to convince Reagan to reverse himself.

On December 7, Devine circulated a memo noting Reagan's three options: preserve the status quo, that is, a ban on all federal employment for the strikers; relent, allowing the strikers to be rehired to their old jobs; or retain the ban on FAA rehiring, but permit strikers to apply for other federal jobs—a middle course in line with what the president himself had floated. The first option, Devine argued, risked portraying the president as uncompassionate. On the other hand, Reagan's supporters would not understand the second option. More crucially, governments abroad would think Reagan inconstant and weak, a factor clearly on the minds of many Reagan advisers. The third option was best, Devine concluded. In a decisive meeting on December 9 at which George Bush, Drew Lewis, Craig Fuller, Fred Fielding, and the Meese-Baker-Deaver Troika were present with Reagan, the president agreed.[86] This could be seen as Reagan's third key formal decision of the sequence, though in another sense, every day from August 5 forward brought pressure to relent and his implicit resolution to stay the course.

Although the decision represented a symbolic moderation of the president's position, it certainly did not satisfy PATCO or the labor movement (with the exception of the Teamsters, who issued a statement commending the president for his magnanimity). In reality, the ongoing federal hiring freeze meant that few jobs outside the FAA were actually available. Asked to comment, Poli called the decision "a cruel hoax." It was, at any rate, not the amnesty PATCO and the AFL-CIO had asked for.[87]

In April 1982, the topic was still heated enough that Reagan was receiving questions from elementary school students about when he would "relent" and rehire the controllers.[88] As late as October 1986, Reagan vetoed a congressional continuing appropriations resolution that provided for the rehiring of the PATCO strikers, calling it "totally unacceptable."[89] He did so on the eve of his departure for the Reykjavic summit with Mikhail Gorbachev. Perhaps the international resonance of his stance was a continuing factor. There would be no mass reinstatement.

Conclusion

It is clear that the PATCO strike was built on a set of miscalculations, though there is still disagreement about the character of the misjudgment. One possibility was that the union believed it could use the threat of a strike to obtain its demands from Ronald Reagan. They were too valuable to the country, and the costs and risks of a strike were too great for the government to allow it to occur. Moreover, the union had endorsed Reagan and believed it had a commitment from Reagan to back its demands. PATCO's 1972 endorsement of Richard Nixon had paid dividends, and PATCO hoped that history would repeat. Five months after the strike collapsed, Poli complained in the pages of the *New York Times* that "It is pathetic that when a politician violates a campaign promise it is accepted as standard practice in this country, but when Federal employees violate their promise not to strike they are castigated as oath breakers and prosecuted as felons."[90]

However, Poli and PATCO leadership seem to have misread Reagan's rather vague letter as a promise to support every detail of PATCO's negotiating position rather than what it arguably was: a promise to take their position into serious consideration and to work for improvements.

In fact, the administration had delivered on many of the items on the October 1980 PATCO list. Remove Langhorne Bond as head of the FAA? Done. Replace Bond with a competent administrator, giving PATCO the opportunity to provide feedback on the nominee? Done. Improve pay, reduce hours, staff up, and upgrade equipment? All these were incorporated into Reagan's exemption of the controllers from the federal hiring freeze and the June 1981 offer Drew Lewis made to PATCO, with Reagan's blessing. It was less than what PATCO asked for, but Reagan addressed almost every item on their October 1980 wish list to some degree—even pay, an issue which he had studiously avoided mentioning in his 1980 letter. It bears repeating that his proposed concession on pay went beyond what the law allowed.

For his part, Reagan, as an experienced labor contract and legislative negotiator, may have mistakenly assumed that the militant new PATCO leadership would understand how these things are supposed to go: if you get a meaningful part of what you asked for, you take the win, go home, and try for more next time. Instead, as PATCO lobbyist and friend of John Leyden, Joseph S. Miller argued later, the union had fallen prey to

> Ego run riot. I had been exposed to egregious hubris before but nothing I had seen in politics or the arts and literature compared to the supreme cocksureness of Bob Poli and his minions. No one could tell them anything. They were invincible and were going to show everyone by humbling the president of the United States. It was madness, of course. One had to experience it to believe it was really happening.[91]

In a 1984 interview, Leyden himself called the Choirboys a "lunatic fringe group that wanted to fight for the sheer sake of fighting" and said the union leaders only talked with each other and "lost sight of the importance of patience and persistence."[92]

PATCO may not only have misinterpreted the nature of Reagan's October 1980 commitment, but the character of his leadership. Reagan himself argued that "members of PATCO were poorly served by their leaders. They apparently thought I was bluffing or playing games when I said controllers who didn't honor the no-strike pledge would lose their jobs and not be rehired."[93] Given the tolerance with which previous presidential administrations had approached past job actions by PATCO and the postal workers, the union was clearly not prepared for Reagan's determination to view the strike as a moral issue. The union hoped that, if it did go to a strike, the government would be forced to quickly fold. Indeed, PATCO members did not believe the FAA would attempt to run the system with fewer than 20 percent of controllers on duty, and one prestrike survey of PATCO members indicated that they thought a strike would be settled within fifteen days.[94] The strike would launch the real negotiations—the ones that would put the finishing touches on the union's claim to be the most successful and most aggressive public sector union in America. In reality, once the unionists crossed the line by breaking their oaths and, in Reagan's view, endangering public safety, negotiations were over. To Reagan it became a matter of principle, and he would not yield.

CHAPTER 4

Political Reaction

The political reaction to the president's decision to fire the striking air traffic controllers was, in general, strongly positive. As one might expect, many other unions and some Democratic officeholders closely affiliated with unions were more critical. Additionally, public opinion was more supportive of the firings than of the ban on all future federal employment by the fired strikers. On balance, though, it quickly became clear that the PATCO militants, from President Robert E. Poli to the Choirboys, had also miscalculated the political reaction to the strike, whether by the public at large, the media, Congress and the courts, or other unions. In short, PATCO inadvertently walked into a political buzzsaw.

Public Opinion

Public opinion and media response had become noticeably cooler to PATCO job actions as the 1970s wore on. More generally, the American public, like the British public, had become increasingly displeased with public employee strikes at all levels, as teachers, postal workers, and police officers walked off the job, disrupting society and (in the case of police and firefighters) arguably endangering lives and property to leverage escalating demands. Public employees sought redress from the effects of stagflation, but taxpayers and those in private employment—that is, most of the country—were suffering, too. Looking across the Atlantic, Americans could not fail to notice that Britain had been virtually crippled by a series of public sector strikes in the winter of 1978–1979. That "winter of discontent" brought Britain to a standstill, led to the fall of the government, and resulted in the election of Margaret Thatcher in May 1979.

The conservative political turn against taxes and big government was exemplified by Thatcher and Reagan, but it was hardly limited to or even originated by them. In America, state elections had seen a turn against taxes, led in 1978 by California's Proposition 13 limiting property taxes, and Congress had just passed Reagan's tax and spending cuts to public acclaim.[1]

Once the strike began, it quickly became clear that PATCO had not grasped how vulnerable its position was. As Michael A. Round observed, "The PATCO strikers failed to establish any support, or any rapport, with the American people, or the Congress. They misjudged the President, as well as their power over the airways."[2]

Reagan, who had a keen sense of such things, undoubtedly believed that most Americans would back him rather than PATCO, and he was right. Public reaction was strongly supportive of Reagan's decision to fire the strikers. On August 4, the second day of the strike, White House phone calls came in at a ratio of nearly twenty to one in favor of the president. By August 6, the fourth day of the strike, phone calls to the White House were still running two to one for the president, while telegrams and mailgrams showed a margin more like ten to one.[3] One congressional office (rather improbably) claimed that mail was running a thousand to one in the president's favor.[4]

More scientifically, from the beginning of the strike, opinion surveys showed public support for the president's position at a ratio of around two to one. The first public poll taken after the strike began, a Gallup/*Newsweek* poll on August 6–7, showed that 57 percent approved of "the way President Reagan is handling the strike." Only 30 percent disapproved.[5] Two-thirds said the strike was wrong, while only 23 percent said it was justified.[6] The survey also indicated that Americans' sympathies lay more with the government than with the strikers—question wording that was more likely to elicit support for the now-fired and bereft strikers—by a 52 to 29 percent margin.[7] The picture did not improve for the strikers after that. Subsequent polls included the following results:

August 10–11 (NBC/AP): A total of 64 percent of respondents indicated approval of the way Reagan was handling the strike versus only 27 percent who disapproved.[8] Two-thirds said the controllers should not be allowed to strike, to only 28 percent who thought they should.[9]

August 11–16: A Harris poll asked, "All in all, in the air traffic controllers strike, are you more in sympathy with the air traffic controllers or the Reagan administration?"—again, wording that tilted toward the union. Yet 51 percent expressed greater sympathy for the administration, to 40 percent for the strikers.[10] Asked another way, seeking approval or disapproval of how Reagan was handling the strike overall, the same poll resulted in approval outrunning disapproval by 58 percent to 39 percent.[11] By a 69 to 27 percent margin, respondents to the Harris poll indicated they supported the firings.[12]

August 14–17: A Gallup poll showed 59 percent approval and 30 percent disapproval of Reagan's handling of the strike.[13] The same poll asked simply, "Should air traffic controllers be permitted to strike, or not?" Only 28 percent said yes, while 68 percent said no.[14]

August 15–22: A Roper survey found that 54 percent thought the government's position was "about right," with another 11 percent thinking the government had not gone far enough. Only 24 percent said the government's position was "too hard."[15] When asked their feelings about the strike itself, 39 percent said "somewhat dissatisfied," 25 percent "angry," and 5 percent "boiling mad"; only 3 percent claimed to be "pleased" and another 6 percent "somewhat satisfied."[16] Nearly two-thirds said they were following the issue "closely."[17]

September 15–17: In response to a Yankelovich, Skelly, and White survey, 57 percent said they "thought more" of Reagan as a result of his handling of the PATCO strike. Only 22 percent said they "thought less" of Reagan.[18]

Thus, according to this series of surveys taken by varying pollsters in the six weeks after the strike began, there was never a point when Reagan was not supported by roughly a two-thirds majority. This support held over time. A survey run by White House pollster Richard Wirthlin in November 1981 showed that 67 percent of Americans supported the president, including three of five blue-collar workers.[19] In mid-December, an NBC survey found roughly the same result, with 64 percent approving.[20] The public, at one point in the 1970s more supportive of labor and even previous PATCO job actions, had turned decisively.

In a *New York Times* column published in January 1982, a few weeks after resigning the presidency of PATCO, Robert E. Poli conceded that the union and the strikers "seemed to go out of their way to solidify public opinion against themselves." Belatedly acknowledging that "no public employee who strikes should expect public support," Poli noted a number of additional factors "amplifying that natural bias." These included:

- "The strike was not only illegal, it was perceived to be an open challenge to a President who had just survived an assassination attempt and was at the peak of his popularity."
- "The strikers were shown as bearded militants with fists raised."
- The union was "hoisted on the petard of its contract demands," as few Americans looked past the call for a $10,000 raise.

All in all, the union was in an unenviable position: As Poli described it, "There was a good guy who stood for principle and order, and a bad guy who represented greed and lawlessness."[21] Other analysts agree. Bernard D. Meltzer and Cass R. Sunstein held that Reagan won the public relations war due to a combination of effective moral argumentation (against lawbreaking and oath-breaking) and successful practical response (a successful FAA contingency plan and absence of an air catastrophe that could be attributed to the PATCO firings).[22] Katherine S. Newman pointed to public perceptions of the strikers as lawless, greedy, and unpatriotic.[23] Arthur B. Shostak and David Skocik highlighted Reagan's recitation of the government employees' no-strike oath in his August 3 remarks, noting that "Reagan's emphasis on the union's lawlessness in repudiating this no-strike oath put PATCO behind the eight ball in the struggle for public sympathy."[24] Adding to the public's dismay may have been lingering frustration over the recent Iranian crisis—as the union's cofounder Jack Maher later explained, "The country was in no mood to be held hostage again, by PATCO or anybody else," and strike opponents adeptly used the "hostage" metaphor against the union.[25] Resentment toward the lengthy Major League Baseball players strike, which had only ended on July 31, also may have affected the atmosphere.

Observers took note not only of public sentiment toward Reagan's strike policies but of trends in his broader presidential job approval rating. Gallup recorded an uptick in Reagan's approval rating from 56 percent in its July 24–27 survey to 59 percent in the July 31–August 3 survey taken as the strike loomed and the president dug in his heels. The next Gallup survey, taken August 14–17 after the mass firings, showed Reagan at 60 percent. Only in September, when the PATCO strike had been superseded by talk of recession and larger-than-expected deficits, did Reagan's numbers recede in the Gallup surveys.[26] ABC News surveys also showed a slight overall bump for the president in this time period, with Reagan's approval rising from 62 percent in late July to 64 percent in late September.[27]

The increases in Reagan's job approval rating in the Gallup and ABC surveys cannot be viewed simply. For one thing, a great deal was going on in this time period that might have elevated Reagan's job approval, including the August 13 signing ceremony for the tax and budget cuts at the president's ranch near Santa Barbara and an August 19 dogfight in which US Navy F-14s shot down two Libyan jets that had fired on them in the Gulf of Sidra. The increases in Reagan's approval in the two surveys were modest. There were also signs that the president's actions were at least somewhat polarizing; not only did Reagan's approval go up in the September ABC poll, his disapproval did, too. Nevertheless, as one would expect given public opinion regarding his actions in the strike itself, Reagan's response to PATCO coincided with a more positive reaction to his presidency as a whole.

While the public was broadly supportive of Reagan's handling of the strike, even at the outset Americans were more divided over whether he should be open to rehiring the fired strikers. In the first poll taken on the subject on August 6–7, Gallup found 44 percent favoring possible rehiring with 42 percent opposed.[28] Once it was clear that the strike had failed and the union shattered, public sentiment became more forgiving. An internal survey conducted in November 1981 by Richard Wirthlin found that 53 percent favored rehiring certain strikers, even if they joined a replacement union.[29] However, when Reagan announced that fired strikers would be allowed to apply for federal jobs but could not be rehired as controllers, it seems that he once again found the sweet spot in public opinion. An NBC poll found that of the roughly one-fourth who had heard of the new policy, 57 percent approved, while only 17 percent disapproved because they thought the controllers should be rehired by the FAA. Another 20 percent believed they should have remained ineligible for all federal employment.[30]

Altogether, a December 1981 poll by the *New York Times* found that, in a year that saw a major tax cut, the first truly significant braking of the federal spending train in decades, a gutsy presidential performance in the midst of an attempted assassination, and a successful faceoff with Moammar Khaddafi, 48 percent of respondents called the PATCO strike their favorite aspect of Reagan's presidential performance that year.[31]

The Coordinate Branches: Congress and the Courts

Researcher Evelyn S. Taylor writes that "Congressional support for Reagan both reflected and acted as a barometer of public sympathy. In the early months of the strike, the White House was besieged with letters from Congressmen, who were besieged by their own constituents, relaying support for the strong anti-strike action taken by the Administration."[32] One example, sent to the president by Congressman Dan Daniel and dated August 3, said, "I am pleased to read that you intend to play hard ball with respect to the air traffic controllers' disregard of the law and public safety."[33]

Even before the strike began, there were numerous signs of congressional hostility to a strike. Then, on day one of the strike (August 3), a long line of senators took to the floor to express their support for Reagan and their unhappiness with the strike.[34] Jake Garn of Utah led off the parade, declaring, "I wish to express in the strongest possible terms my anger with the Nation's air traffic controller strike." Garn went on to contend that "what the Professional Air Traffic Controllers Association [sic] has wrought is a class case of employee greediness.... I cannot emphasize strongly enough that this strike is illegal." Following Garn was Nancy Landon Kassebaum of Kansas, daughter of 1936 Republican presidential candidate Alf Landon. Landon predicted that the "illegal action will do nothing to further the goals of increased pay and change in working conditions of the controllers. That proposal which was forwarded to them was fair and equitable. I believe that the Administration should be praised for its reaction to this illegality in the strike that was called this morning." Mack Mattingly of Georgia piled on, commending Garn and Landon and calling "correct" the forty-eight-hour ultimatum delivered by the president. Mattingly went on to criticize Robert Poli, cite Reagan's action as a warning against strikes by other federal employee unions, and say, "I suggest to [Poli] and those people who do not show up for work in 48 hours to please find other employment because the American people will not be held hostage."

Bob Packwood of Oregon endorsed the views of his colleagues, noted that the strike—carried on in defiance of a court order—was illegal, and reminded listeners that "This is a time when tremendous efforts are being exercised by the executive branch and Congress to slow down inflation," a goal at odds with PATCO's extravagant demands. He also reminded the strikers that any new contract including a pay raise would have to be approved by Congress. Majority Leader Howard Baker of Tennessee put the president's statement of that morning into the record, saying, "It is correct, and I support it." Garn noted that at least two other senators, Chiles of Florida and Hollings of South Carolina, had wanted to make anti-strike statements but were unable to attend the Senate because of flight delays caused by the strike.

Later in the day, after a long discussion ending in final passage of the Economic Recovery Tax Act (ERTA), Senator John Stennis of Mississippi took the floor. After relating a pleasant experience he had visiting air traffic controllers at work in the past, he pivoted to say that none of that visit made any difference today. In the view of Senator Stennis, firing the strikers would be appropriate given their no-strike oath and the fact that "the lives of countless of thousands of innocent people are imperiled by the hour with reference to the functions of these controllers." By the end of the day, eight senators had spoken strongly against the strike, including two conservative Republicans (Garn and Mattingly), three moderate Republicans (Baker, Kassebaum, Packwood), and three southern Democrats (Chiles, Hollings, Stennis). No one had risen to defend it, or even try to rationalize it. The first day of the strike was the last day before August recess, and the Senate adjourned until September 9.

On the House side, August 3 was consumed by final reading of the conference committee report on ERTA. The next day, just prior to the start of the House's August recess, Ted Weiss of New York acknowledged that the strike was one of the most inconvenient of recent memory, and that it was "also illegal." However, "Those facts do not excuse the incredible overreaction of President Reagan, who obviously intends to bust the union." Because both firing the strikers and decertifying the union would be counterproductive, "The president's attempts at union busting could turn an unmanageable situation into an impossible one." Weiss was followed by Mary Rose Oakar of Ohio, who also pronounced a pox on both houses—the strike and Reagan's reaction. An extended strike, she noted, would do severe harm to the economy. Consequently, she said, "I strongly urge the FAA and PATCO to return to the negotiating table." Oakar, as chair of the House Subcommittee on Compensation and Employee Benefits, offered her good offices to help resolve the conflict.

After a brief interlude, Republican Donald L. Ritter followed the two Democrats to announce that he was planning to propose a "sense of the Congress" resolution stating that the strike was illegal and must end immediately. Congressman Lawrence Coughlin, the ranking minority member on the House Transportation Appropriations Subcommittee, expressed "outrage" over the air traffic controllers' strike. Both travelers and government, he complained, were "held hostage by this illegal action" taken by the union on behalf of a set of contract demands that "flies in the face of reality." Conservatives were robust in their opposition to the strike, while normally prolabor members offered a mixed assessment and hedged their bets. Later that day, John Conyers (D-MI) indicated he was introducing legislation (H.R. 4375) that would have legalized the PATCO strike by providing all federal employees with the right to strike.[35] Of the five Representatives, Conyers was the farthest left by a wide margin and served as the exception that proved the rule. In a letter to the *New York Times* published on August 7, Conyers elaborated to a national reading audience that "The idea that Government employees are different from other types of workers is without foundation" and that it was a national embarrassment that public strikes in the United States were treated differently than private sector strikes.[36]

It was clear, however, that Conyers's view was not the majority's, and his legislation never progressed. On the contrary, an August 10 *Newsweek* report stated that "a group of Senate and House members has vowed that Congress will not support any settlement that results from an illegal walkout."[37] The Associated Press concluded in mid-August that "Congress has shown no inclination" to pass legislation requiring the administration to rehire the strikers, while noting that Drew Lewis promised a presidential veto in the unlikely event such legislation was actually enacted.[38] Most members were not anxious to back a large raise for controllers after having just voted to trim Social Security, school lunches, and a score of other popular domestic programs. Even prolabor members were "less than ready to fight for a union that was engaged in an illegal strike."[39] In or out of Congress, elected Democrats were evenly divided between those who offered vague sympathy to the strikers and those who condemned the strike. Even Detroit Mayor Coleman Young, a former UAW autoworker, said the strikers were "holding the nation hostage," that they were making "outrageous" demands, and that Reagan was a "hero" for his stand.[40]

At least nominally the most powerful person in the House, Speaker Tip O'Neill remained circumspect.[41] He expressed sympathy for the strikers, criticized Reagan for refusing to compromise, and urged the president to rehire the strikers. He also noted publicly that PATCO had endorsed Reagan and was now reaping the reward. However, as former O'Neill staffer Chris Matthews would later write, when the speaker was commenting behind the scenes, "Tip was forced to acknowledge the political muscle Reagan was displaying."[42] He privately urged Robert Poli to postpone the strike deadline, never endorsed the strike, and did not exert himself to protect the strikers. His lukewarm (or as Matthews called it, "layered") response to the strike is evidenced by the fact that the PATCO strike makes no appearance in either O'Neill's own memoirs or his foremost political biography.[43]

While there remained a significant number of supporters of Reagan's policy toward the strikers, by late 1981 many had changed their tone, expressing concern for air safety and for the hardships experienced by the strikers and their families. Both Democrats as well as Republicans such as Guy Molinari and Jack Kemp argued for clemency. Later in the decade, there were some legislative efforts in Congress to fund reinstatement of strikers in air traffic control positions, but the Department of Transportation and Office of Personnel Management opposed the efforts, and most went nowhere.[44] The only time such a provision made it into legislation that passed both houses (in 1986), Reagan vetoed it. All in all, one AFL-CIO official attributed PATCO's disaster in part to its disdain for Congress, which turned on the union when it mattered most: "We'd *always* used Congress. . . . *They* threw it away."[45]

Courts had already ruled against PATCO and had even berated the Carter administration in 1979 for not taking a stronger stand against illegal PATCO "job actions." The Air Transport Association (ATA) directly warned PATCO that based on the standing injunction of 1970, it would seek legal remedy in the event of a strike.[46] On June 18, federal Judge Thomas C. Platt refused PATCO's request that the 1970 injunction be vacated.

When the strike finally came, federal courts followed through. In short order, courts ordered PATCO to pay $28.8 million in damages to the ATA. They also imposed heavy daily fines, which judges eventually reduced when it became clear that the administration would not let strikers come back to work even if they wanted to. The damages and fines added up to an amount much greater than PATCO's assets. The beating that PATCO took in court began on day one of the strike, when federal Judge Harold H. Greene in Washington, DC found the union in contempt of court and began imposing fines that could total nearly $5 million in a week. Greene's order stated, "It is clear on this record that the harm threatened in this situation is of the highest magnitude."[47] The next day, Judge Platt in Brooklyn assigned a fine of $100,000 per hour on PATCO for violating the 1970 anti-strike injunction. By August 5, Robert Poli admitted the union had lost access to its $3 million strike fund, impounded to pay the fines.

Federal courts also had to process the Justice Department prosecutions of individuals the department had identified as strike leaders. There were a variety of resolutions to the charges. Some PATCO defendants reached plea bargains, while some were convicted and sentenced to probation, fines, or jail time ranging from a few days to a few months. A small number were able to convince judges that their prosecution was impermissibly selective. A legal analysis by Bernard D. Meltzer and Cass R. Sunstein notes that "under current law the executive may single out violators who have been most vocal in resistance to the law whose violation is in question." However, selective prosecution cannot be used to chill legitimate constitutional rights, though Meltzer and Sunstein found this defense "unpersuasive" under the circumstances. Such a defense failed in court most of the time, but it did succeed in a handful of cases.[48] The prosecutions of alleged PATCO strike leaders continued until 1983.

Courts played a role in the decertification of PATCO, as well. On August 14, at the behest of the administration, Administrative Law Judge John Fenton recommended that the Federal Labor Relations Authority (FLRA) decertify the union, setting the decertification process in motion. The resulting October 22, 1981 decertification of PATCO by the FLRA was appealed by the union in federal court. However, the US Circuit Court of Appeals for the District of Columbia dismissed the appeal on June 11, 1982, driving the final nail into PATCO's coffin.

Strike supporters also played offense in the courts, but to no avail. In November 1981, a coalition of labor leaders and advocacy groups, including UAW's Douglas Fraser and consumer advocate Ralph Nader, sued in federal court to force the Reagan administration to rehire the fired strikers. The suit made no effort to defend the strike per se but contended that failure to rehire trained controllers posed an unacceptable threat to public safety. The FAA called the suit "groundless," and fifteen US House members countersued. The Fraser-Nader suit was dismissed in US District Court a month later.[49]

Media

In a forty-year strike anniversary article, the World Wide Socialist Web glumly but correctly summed that the news media, "whether liberal or conservative, overwhelmingly condemned the air traffic controllers."[50] To begin with, print media was generally unsupportive of the strike. The

New York Times, which rarely agreed with the Reagan administration but also had a history of criticizing PATCO job actions, called the administration's offer to PATCO "more than reasonable."[51] Once the strike began, the *Times* editorialized that the merits of PATCO's demands were "dubious," that Reagan's ultimatum was "appropriate," and that "the controllers have no legal right to promote their interests by damaging the national economy." A retreat by Reagan, the *Times* predicted, would invite other government employees to exploit their leverage. All in all, "Living temporarily without air service is a heavy burden. Restoring it on the controllers' terms could be a disaster."[52] The *Washington Post,* another frequent Reagan critic, commented that "In a year of belt tightening throughout government, it is a little difficult to make a sound case for even the pay increases the controllers have already been offered."[53] Moreover, the *Post* calculated, "If one union, whose members work directly for Mr. Reagan, were now to achieve a spectacular wage increase through an illegal strike, that would be the end of the Reagan economic program. Investors, bankers and borrowers would all immediately conclude that, whatever his rhetoric, the Reagan Administration was not serious about reducing inflation. That's why Mr. Reagan now has to stand absolutely fast."[54]

The *New York Daily News* held that the strikers "deserve what is coming to them," declaring that:

> Except for a handful of labor leaders and professional civil-rights pleaders, public support for the President appears overwhelming. To the public, as to Reagan, the dispute ceased to be a controversy over pay and working conditions when the controllers walked out. At that moment, it became a test of whether public employees can flout the law with impunity.
>
> It was a challenge from which Reagan dared not flinch. Concessions or compromises would only have emboldened other federal unions to hold essential government services hostage to the demands....
>
> The inconveniences will be a small price to pay for upholding a principle the very heart and soul of a democratic society based on law.[55]

In the early days of the strike, the *Atlanta Journal-Constitution* offered its opinion that "The Reagan administration is to be commended for its hard-nosed attitude toward striking controllers." In Portland, the *Oregon Journal* similarly expressed the view that "Air traffic controllers ought to fall into that category of public employment that should be barred legally from striking because it is a vital public service."[56] The *Chicago Tribune* noted that the strike "has produced silence from administration critics, embarrassment for the labor movement, and hostility toward the controllers. Its end result is likely to be another batch of headlines saying, 'Ronald Reagan wins another one.'"[57] The *Wall Street Journal* counseled there was "no room for compromise." If Reagan were to back off, the *Journal* predicted, "both respect for the law and his presidency will suffer."[58] From the heartland, the *Fort Worth Star-Telegram* pulled no punches. After dismissing as "hogwash" the controllers' argument that they should be equated with Poland's Solidarity movement, the *Star-Telegram* opined that "After watching the antics on television and reading the remarks in the newspaper of the strikers, an air traveler is inclined to believe he is safer without those self-centered controllers."[59] Other papers concurred, including the Charleston (South Carolina) *News & Courier*, the *Oklahoma City Times*, the *Pittsburgh Press*, the *St. Louis Globe-Democrat*, the Charlotte (North Carolina) *Observer*, the *Seattle Times*, the *Manchester Union-Leader*, the *Richmond Times-Dispatch*, and the *Dallas Morning News*.[60]

The *Boston Globe* was more circumspect, seeming to mourn the end of labor solidarity in the United States but observing that "President Reagan did what he says was the necessary thing, what surely is the popular thing and what may be the right thing." The *Globe* editorial, however ambivalent, concluded with the famous quote from Calvin Coolidge: "There is no right to strike against the public safety by anybody, any time."[61] Two months later, the *Globe* editorialized that "For the Reagan Administration, the PATCO strike has been a means to send important signals to employers and employees in the public sector: Strikes have no place in deciding the allocation of public funds and no-strike pledges mean what they say.... Teaching PATCO (and others) a lesson was essential. Eliminating the union by decertification is at least arguably warranted." But, the *Globe* argued, the fired strikers should be given a way back to their old jobs.⁶² A few others also took an evenhanded approach, calling for more communication, new negotiations, or binding arbitration. The Gary, Indiana *Post* was a rare paper that was more sympathetic to the strikers than to the government.⁶³

On the West Coast, William Randolph Hearst Jr. took to the pages of the Sunday *San Francisco Chronicle and Examiner* to survey the strike. While disclaiming any intention to take sides, Hearst argued that as the chief executive officer of the nation, Reagan "had the solemn duty of reminding his countrymen of their obligation to obey the laws of the land. One of those laws says it is illegal for public employees to walk away from their jobs." He then went on to quote, at length and approvingly, Reagan's August 3 press statement.⁶⁴ By the end of August, the *Sunday Chronicle and Examiner* was calling, like the *Globe* and other papers, for carefully circumscribed clemency for the fired controllers. Reagan, the editorial urged, has made his valid point; illegal strikes will not be tolerated. Now was the time for magnanimity.⁶⁵ Down the coast, the *Los Angeles Times* struck a similar chord in mid-September, calling the strike a "headstrong gamble" lost by the controllers. "The President has made his point," the *Times* editorialized, calling it an "undeniable fact" that "the air traffic controllers violated a pledge and the law by striking." Compassion was the next order of business.⁶⁶

The broadcast media, where most Americans received their news, was no more sympathetic than the print media and were probably more influential. David Morgan, who interviewed participants in both PATCO and the administration, wrote that both sides agreed: "'Lewis, not Poli, won the battle of the television screens.' The mass media were important in reinforcing the undoubtedly strong hand of the Administration."⁶⁷ Lewis started each day at 5:30 a.m., going on all three major networks to repeat the same themes: the skies were safe, PATCO's demands were exorbitant, and the strike was illegal.

In radio broadcasting, one of the biggest audiences of the time belonged to Paul Harvey, whose commentary was syndicated over the ABC radio network. Harvey strongly and repeatedly criticized PATCO and the strike, praising Reagan for giving the union what it deserved. "As industry's tycoons of the Thirties got their wings clipped, labor's leaders in the Eighties are getting their wings clipped. Not because of any class-related antagonism, but because any excess, ultimately, is inevitably its own undoing."[68] To Harvey, Reagan was simply restoring balance.

In the world of journals of opinion, the center-left *New Republic* expressed skepticism that Reagan had been bargaining in good faith and posited that some of PATCO's grievances were legitimate, but acknowledged that "PATCO members undid their moral claims by going on strike." In a tone of sorrow rather than anger, the publication held that the strike might have been averted with more accommodation on both sides. However, at the end of the day, it declared that "the strike was wrong" and, like the *Boston Globe*, quoted what it called one of Calvin Coolidge's "few intelligent public utterances": "There is no right to strike against the public safety."[69]

As one might expect, on the right, Reagan's favorite publication, William F. Buckley's *National Review*, assessed shortly after the strike began that

> In this "contest" the only things Reagan has going for him are the law, economics, total public support, and the practical leverage inherent in the fact that despite the strike three-fourths of scheduled flights were operating. On top of all that, Reagan had the opportunity to make a necessary and popular political point. Public employees cannot be allowed to strike.... It is a point worth making and long overdue.[70]

Two months after the strike began, *National Review* published a lengthy piece by columnist James Kilpatrick which laid out his interpretation of the long-developing crisis with the controllers, putting the strike in the context of growing public sector union power in America. Calling the PATCO strike a "blow for tyranny," Kilpatrick applauded Reagan's firmness but noted that it would have only a temporary effect if Americans did not take advantage of the opportunity to wake up to the broader threat.[71]

After the initial endorsements of Reagan's policy, significant media support arose for the idea of rehiring the strikers. Haynes Johnson, for example, suggested that Reagan had revealed himself as "harsh, unyielding, almost vengeful and mean-spirited" by hewing to the original firings.[72] Perhaps most notable was a column written by William Raspberry for the *Washington Post* on December 7. Admitting the strike was illegal, Raspberry nonetheless called for amnesty, noting America's tradition of being "uncompromising in war and generous in victory."[73]

David Morgan contrasts a weak PATCO public relations strategy with a disciplined administration strategy, and notes that the major networks and newspapers tended to assign their "labor beat" reporters to the story, a contingent of journalists who were "not particularly sympathetic" to the union. Morgan argues that a better media presentation by PATCO would not have changed the ultimate outcome, but might have improved PATCO's prospects on the margins (for example, regarding selective rehiring). Overall, he concludes that Reagan's high public standing was critical: "Media coverage reflected a judgment by reporters and editors that the American public had spoken decisively nine months previously—and that it was not a time to question that judgment, or assist PATCO in its defiance of it."[74]

Unions and Other Interest Groups

In his essay attempting to explain the failure of the strike, Robert Poli cited organized labor as one of the key contributors to the strike's failure. According to Poli, while PATCO did not expect other unions to join the strike, it did expect that "some of our 'brothers' in the trade union movement would not go out of their way to hurt us. They did."[75]

For many reasons, PATCO found itself isolated from the rest of the labor movement. It was pushing beyond the limits of the law, and it was doing so on behalf of demands that many rank-and-file union members around the country found excessive. The highest-paid federal workers were walking out in pursuit of a $10,000 raise at a time when blue-collar union jobs might only pay $10,000 or $15,000 a year. Furthermore, the 1970 injunction against PATCO prohibited anyone else "acting in concert" with PATCO from encouraging or aiding a strike, a clause that many union officials felt might put them at risk if they went too far on PATCO's behalf.[76] PATCO's support of Reagan in 1980 and its historic tendency to cross picket lines by other airport unions also did not endear it to its brothers and sisters in the labor movement.[77]

Not least, PATCO had jumped into the strike against a popular president without consulting the AFL-CIO—one Drew Lewis aide claimed that "we talked to the AFL more than Poli did"—and some union leaders such as United Auto Workers president Douglas Fraser feared that PATCO had carelessly walked into a situation that could redound against the entire labor movement. AFL-CIO insiders later said the illegality of the strike and Reagan's "political muscle" were the two most important factors behind labor's caution. Consequently, while labor criticized Reagan's firing of the strikers, and more harshly criticized his unwillingness to reinstate them, it exerted itself very little in defense of the strike itself. Despite Poli's plea of August 7, few unions instructed their members to honor PATCO picket lines or offered any kind of financial support to the strikers until the strike was already beaten. A spokesman for the American Federation of Government Employees summed up the situation when he said his union was "condoning supporting [PATCO] in any way we can, morally, legally, but not to walk out on our jobs."[78]

Although Lane Kirkland and the AFL-CIO issued public statements supporting the strikers, the support was half-hearted. As discussed in chapter three, Kirkland privately proposed to Reagan that the president rehire most of the strikers, that Poli resign from the PATCO presidency, and that Kirkland himself would declare Reagan had done the right thing. Kirkland's idea never gained traction in the White House and was rejected by PATCO. In public, Kirkland called Reagan's decision to fire the strikers "harsh and brutal" and "out of all proportion." The AFL-CIO issued a statement supporting PATCO and urging the administration to "call off its punitive measure." Overall, while the labor movement expressed support for PATCO, "all were careful to avoid the appearance of sanctioning an illegal strike." Kirkland, for example, skirted the issue, saying, "I respect the law, but events here and elsewhere in the world have demonstrated that when working people feel a deep sense of grievance they will exercise what I think is a basic human right to withhold their services, not to work under conditions they no longer find tolerable."[79] This ambivalence was reflected as well in Kirkland's declaration that member unions of the AFL-CIO would have to decide for themselves what to do in respect to honoring PATCO picket lines or offering other assistance. Even further, Erik Loomis claims in *A History of America in Ten Strikes* that privately, the AFL-CIO "sent out letters to its unions banning them from engaging in any secondary strikes or more radical actions to support the controllers."⁸⁰

At a meeting of the AFL-CIO executive council day the strike began, William Winpisinger, president of the Machinists Union, offered to pull his airport-serving members out of work—effectively shutting down airports across America—if the other unions present at the meeting would also pull their people out. Instead, the group declined to call for action until there was a direct conversation with Poli. It was becoming clear, Shostak and Skocik later wrote, that "few labor leaders believed their rank and file felt strongly for the controllers or their strike."⁸¹ Kirkland made his statement and proposed that PATCO and the White House accept former Gerald Ford's Labor Secretary W. J. Usery as a mediator, an idea that went nowhere.

The AFL-CIO did establish a fund that ultimately disbursed $840,000 for PATCO strikers who were experiencing financial distress. The Independent Federation of Flight Attendants, American Federation of Teachers, Winpisinger's Machinists, and the Maritime Engineers Beneficial Association (PATCO's parent union), took out newspaper advertisements supporting PATCO and provided the controllers with free supplies and meeting places.⁸²

The AFL-CIO had already announced a major march and rally in Washington, DC on September 19 in response to Reagan's conservative agenda. Now "Solidarity Day" became about the PATCO strike. An estimated 250,000 people representing one hundred unions and one hundred and fifty other organizations attended, perhaps "the largest U.S. labor march ever held." However, "One saw considerable rhetoric and chest-beating—and little else."⁸³ The energy behind the pro-PATCO moment dissipated rapidly, and less than a month after "Solidarity Day" the AFL-CIO executive council met with Poli and told him they saw the strike as a lost cause. At most, if labor was fortunate, they might salvage a few of the strikers' jobs. A month after that, on November 19, the AFL-CIO convention approved a resolution condemning the "brutal punishment" inflicted on the strikers and demanding that Reagan "return these workers to their jobs," but little came of it. The convention rejected a call for a one-day general strike by all AFL-CIO affiliated unions to support

PATCO. Kirkland reported receiving pressure from union activists, but answered that "It's easy to be a midnight gin militant and call for a general strike, but if you're a responsible leader you have to appraise the consequences."[84]

In the AFL-CIO, one union stood out as particularly crucial to PATCO's goals—the Air Line Pilots Association (ALPA). If ALPA either explicitly honored the picket line or backed the strike practically by refusing to fly on safety grounds, the strike might have been unstoppable. However, ALPA officials not only did not back the controllers but seemed to go out of their way to undercut the controllers' position by affirming that the government's contingency plan was working safely. Poli singled out ALPA as particularly damaging to PATCO's cause, writing that "While most other aviation industry unions gave us at least moral support, ALPA went down and below the call of duty attempting to hurt us. ALPA members seemed to fall over each other to get before TV cameras and proclaim the air traffic control system safe."[85] Other PATCO supporters called ALPA "perhaps the biggest sellout" of the episode.[86] ALPA President J. J. O'Donnell, a longtime friend of John Leyden, may have held Poli's 1980 treachery against him; Willis J. Nordlund contends that "the coup that led Poli to the PATCO presidency left a bad taste" in O'Donnell's mouth.[87] While O'Donnell said he would not cross a picket line, he said he would leave it up to each pilot to decide whether to respect the PATCO picket lines. Unlike other members of the AFL-CIO executive council, meeting in Chicago at the outset of the strike, he declined to join the picket line at O'Hare Airport.

Among pilots more generally, the predominant sentiment seemed to be anger against the controllers. They understood that the substantial slowdown in air traffic caused by the strike would lead to thousands of pilots furloughed by the airlines. ALPA privately monitored air safety issues in the wake of the strike and found an increase in near-midair collisions, but O'Donnell kept the reports confidential. Although some pilots privately expressed concern, only two pilots exercised their right not to fly found in Federal Air Regulation 91.3. On August 18, the ALPA executive board met and unanimously concluded that the skies were safe. The next day, O'Donnell held a press conference and declared that "I can say without equivocation the air traffic control system in this country is safe. If it were not safe, we would be the first ones to speak out."[88] At the end of his press conference, O'Donnell suggested that Reagan should accept his victory in the standoff and agree to rehire controllers who admitted their mistake. Anger against PATCO was so strong, though, that Delta and Eastern Airlines pilots approved resolutions denouncing O'Donnell's suggestion.[89] Altogether, ALPA, which could have provided important support to PATCO, actually worked against it.

As one labor historian points out, the American unions were not just divided, one from another—PATCO striking, ALPA opposed, AFL-CIO lukewarm except for Machinists and a few others, and so forth. There was also an important crosscutting division within the labor movement more generally—labor activists who were more pro-strike, and rank-and-file members, who were less supportive or even hostile.[90] Arthur B. Shostak and David Skocik conclude that "PATCO was denied decisive all-out labor support that might have forced Reagan to seek a face-saving settlement ... Instead, understandably reluctant to take on a new U.S. President by going all-out in support of an illegal and instantly unpopular strike, the labor movement fussed and fumed, finally to stand exposed as a paper tiger."[91] Or, as editorialists of *The New Republic* drily remarked in late August, labor support for the strikers "remained confined to the mimeograph machine."[92]

There was actually more agitation among unions abroad than there was at home. Most importantly, Canadian air traffic controllers briefly refused to clear American planes in protest, which had the effect of closing down routes over the North Atlantic. PATCO Executive Vice President Robert E. Meyer had believed international support, especially from Canada, would be crucial to the success of the strike.[93] The Canadian protest lasted two days, until the US government made it clear that, if necessary, it would open up the routes using AWACS planes and US Navy missile cruisers staffed with FAA controllers. At the same time, Drew Lewis and J. Lynn Helms worked to coordinate response with the Canadian government, which suspended twenty-nine controllers and sought judicial injunctions against the Canadian Air Traffic Controllers Association (CATCA). A boycott of US flights by Portuguese, French, and New Zealand controllers was similarly short-lived and had little effect. When the International Federation of Air Traffic Controllers' Associations (IFATCA) briefly considered endorsing action supporting the PATCO strike, despite the fact that PATCO had left the federation some years before, the Reagan administration lobbied governments to prevent a boycott of US flights. As part of this effort, Reagan also announced that he would delay implementation of a Civil Air Board rule against collusive price setting on transatlantic flights that had been strongly opposed by European governments. The lobbying worked, and IFATCA stayed out of the PATCO dispute.[94] In the end, Meyer's gambit failed.

Outside of labor, the most politically important organizations were either opposed to the strike or silent. The ACLU was an exception, issuing a statement on August 3 asserting that the oath taken by controllers not to strike was unconstitutional, as it required them to abjure a basic right (the right to strike).[95] On the other hand, as in past PATCO job actions, the Air Transport Association, the advocacy group for airlines, worked hard against the strike. The ATA coordinated with FAA administrator J. Lynn Helms to mobilize member airlines behind the FAA's strike plan. Despite (or perhaps because of) suffering large financial losses, airline executives backed Reagan, contrary to PATCO's expectations. The chairman of American Airlines, for example, thanked the president for "reestablishing respect for law and controlling inflation." These steps, he asserted, would lead to "a business environment in which the temporary losses we suffer now can be more than fully recouped."[96] Trans World Airlines spokesman Ken Johnson talked up air travel, saying, "I think more passengers are coming out, realizing that people will not get stranded.... We can still handle air traffic. There is no problem at all."[97] Behind the scenes, some analysts reported that the stronger airlines welcomed the strike and the firing of controllers because it gave them the opportunity to restructure and streamline their operations in the new environment of airline deregulation.[98]

The US Chamber of Commerce declared its support for Reagan's response to the PATCO strike on August 4. "We fully support the president's actions," said Robert T. Thompson, "Despite all the rhetoric, one fact is clear. The strike action taken by members of the union at the urging of their leadership is in direct violation of federal law and the express orders of federal courts."[99] Even the American Bar Association passed a resolution supporting the firing, though its subcommittee of labor attorneys objected.[100] When Vice President George Bush and Attorney General William French Smith spoke at the ABA convention on August 11, both received applause by denouncing the PATCO strike. Smith would later write that the occasion was the first time he could remember receiving a standing ovation from the ABA.[101]

Conclusion

Ronald Reagan's decision to fire the PATCO strikers worked for the president because, at bottom, a large majority of Americans supported it. At the same time, the other branches of the federal government, which could have challenged the policy, supported it or positively aided its enforcement. The national media, on balance, was unsympathetic to the strikers. The union movement, which also could have posed serious problems for Reagan had it coalesced aggressively behind PATCO, did not do so, while key business groups backed Reagan. Supporters of the president's policy were vehement, while labor supporters—whether prolabor members of Congress, the center-left media, or the AFL-CIO—were at best ambivalent.

Was the public at large supportive of the president partly because prolabor members of Congress and other unions were not strongly behind the strike? Or were many Democratic members of Congress, the normally-liberal media, and the AFL-CIO reluctant to confront Reagan precisely because the president and his PATCO policy were so popular? Probably more the latter than the former. Reagan's political strength heavily shaped the environment and became self-reinforcing. After all, the earliest polls already showed a large majority approving his PATCO policy before it was clear what other unions or the media would do. The public polls also showed that Reagan grew stronger as the month of August wore on, though the objective facts of restored air travel and demonstrated air safety were arguably more salient to the public than the responses of secondary institutions. However, public opinion writ large and secondary institutions doubtless affected each other, at least to some degree. The fact that Reagan's popular support affected Congress, media, and unions did not exclude these groups from also having an effect on Reagan's popularity.

What is clear is that, taken together, the responses of the political system to Reagan's decision to fire the PATCO strikers provided important support to the decision. Throughout his presidency, Reagan often sensed rather astutely what traffic the American political bridge could bear. In the dispute with PATCO, Reagan's political instinct served him well. Just as the illegality of the strike seemed to drive Reagan's decision, it also seemed to drive much of the political reaction outside the White House, from conservative fury to liberal ambivalence. Supportive reaction by the public created the conditions that made it possible for Reagan's policy to be sustained. At the same time, there is no evidence that Reagan's policy was controlled by public opinion, except at the margins. The decision to fire the striking controllers was made before there was firm information on what the political reaction would be. When the rest of the political system moved in the direction of clemency, Reagan took a visible step to appease it without fundamentally relenting.

CHAPTER 5

Consequences

There were two immediate consequences of Reagan's decision to fight the PATCO strike. First, PATCO itself was destroyed; its strike was broken and the union itself was soon decertified and bankrupted by fines. Second, the nation experienced a short-term disruption of air travel, though much less disruption than many had feared (or the union had hoped). Accompanying this disruption was some economic dislocation, especially (though unevenly felt) in the airline industry. If this was all there was to the story, the moment might be written off as a highly dramatic and intense episode of little long-term significance to anyone but the fired strikers and their families, many of whom struggled for years with financial and emotional difficulties.[1] According to a 1986 study by the General Accounting Office, among fired PATCO strikers:

- Seven in ten had not yet found a job that matched their prestrike income.
- One in three qualified for food stamps.
- One in five worked entry-level jobs in clerical, sales, service, or unskilled manual labor.
- Almost one in seven had lost their homes.[2]

Fired strikers had the opportunity to appeal their dismissals to the Merit Systems Protection Board on the grounds that they were coerced into joining the strike or were mistakenly counted absent from work after the forty-eight-hour deadline had expired. Almost every fired striker appealed, more than 10,000 altogether. Eventually, around 350 won their appeals, but two years later only about one-third of those had actually been taken back by the FAA.[3] Not until the Clinton administration was the presidential order barring reemployment by the FAA rescinded. On August 12, 1993, a joint statement was issued by the US Department of Transportation and the Office of Personnel Management: "While the administration does not condone illegal job actions in the federal government, reasonable people would agree that after 12 years former air traffic controllers should be able to apply for employment." It was a testament to the ongoing symbolic power of Reagan's decision that the order went out while President Clinton was on vacation, and not under his name. Within a year, 40 percent of those fired had applied for their old jobs. However, controller jobs were few and far between, former controllers were given no preference, and two years after the DOT/OPM order, only thirty-seven fired strikers had been rehired. By 2006, that number had slowly climbed to around eight hundred and fifty, still only 7 percent of those who had been fired.[4]

The dissolution of PATCO on July 25, 1982 did not mean that the grievances controllers harbored against the FAA vanished. Stresses continued, and it was not long before the controllers began forming new organizations to advance their interests. A week after the demise of PATCO, union veterans formed USATCO, the United States Air Traffic Controllers Organization. USATCO disbanded in 1984, the same year controllers at the Washington Center formed the National Air Traffic Controllers Association (NATCA). NATCA went truly national in 1986. A year later a certification election was held, and more than 70 percent of controllers approved naming NATCA their official union representation. In recognition of past disputes, the NATCA leadership promised to work within the law. In 1996, Jack Maher, one of the founders of the original PATCO, launched PATCO Local 6881 (referring to the years of original PATCO activity, 1968 to 1981), affiliated with the AFL-CIO, and organized a number of privatized control towers at small airports.[5]

Aside from the strike's effect on the union itself, air travel was seriously affected; the FAA reported a year later that air traffic was running at 83 percent of its prestrike norm.[6] Pan Am departures were still down by 31 percent and TWA by 17 percent. While many air carriers took advantage of the slowdown to restructure, it was fatal to Braniff Airlines, which had been struggling seriously before the strike and went under in May 1982.[7]

The short-term costs of the strike to the economy were estimated to run more than $50 million a day, a sizeable figure, but less than anticipated and not catastrophic in a $3 trillion economy.[8] The vast bulk of that cost—$35 million a day—was borne by the airlines, who clearly saw the cost as a worthwhile price to pay to break the union. It was also estimated at the time that the cost of training a new cohort of controllers might reach $1.3 billion.

There was no airline crash that was officially deemed attributable to air traffic control errors, though PATCO claimed that the crash of Air Florida Flight 90 into the Potomac River in January 1982 could be blamed on an overworked controller taking too long to give permission for takeoff in icy conditions. There was some evidence that safety had deteriorated in the immediate aftermath of the strike. The Aviation Safety Institute reported that in the first week after the strike began, there was one systems error per hour between 6 a.m. and 10 p.m., compared with one and a half per day before the strike. In December 1981, the National Transportation Safety Board released a report on air safety which raised possible concerns about the poststrike system but was generally positive about air safety.[9] PATCO claimed that near-midair collisions increased, but these did not translate into actual collisions. The FAA disputed PATCO's assertion, claiming that in the first two weeks of the strike there were actually only about half as many near-collisions as there had been one year before.[10] Either claim was plausible: overworked and inexperienced controllers may have led to an increase in near-misses, while reduced density of air traffic could have led to a reduction in them. In any event, there was no rash of airline crashes as predicted by PATCO.

Instead, four sets of long-term consequences—economic, coalitional, institutional, and international—made Reagan's PATCO decision truly significant over the next four decades and beyond.

Economic Consequences

It is now widely recognized that Reagan's handling of the PATCO strike had a long-term impact on labor-management relations in America. Indeed, this consequence is probably the one most often remarked upon, though often simplistically. Union officials at the time predicted that the firings "could well be the opening salvo" of an administration war against labor.[11] Douglas Fraser of the United Auto Workers feared that PATCO had carelessly walked into a situation that could harm organized labor for years to come. At the meeting of the AFL-CIO executive council on August 3, the first day of the strike, Fraser perceived that "This could do massive damage to the labor movement." Joseph A. McCartin, looking back after three decades, concluded that Fraser was right: "No strike since the advent of the New Deal damaged the U.S. labor movement more."[12]

This was most clearly true in relations between government and the public employee unions, which were the focus of Reagan's ire in 1981. Atlanta Mayor Maynard Jackson took the lead in firing striking public workers in the 1970s.[13] However, Willis J. Nordlund observes that "August 3, 1981 is a pivotal day in federal sector labor-management relations" because "it is the first time that the Federal government destroyed a federal union."[14]

Union leaders like American Federation of Government Employees (AFGE) president Ken Blaylock and postal workers union leader Moe Biller noted the change in atmosphere; Blaylock's union lost 30 percent of its members between 1980 and 1987. McCartin writes that:

> In the two years following the strike, the number of federal workers covered by union contracts suffered its biggest drop since the government began keeping track in 1963. Agencies also became noticeably tougher in negotiations. When the Postal Services took a hard line during negotiations in 1984, observers attributed it to the precedent set by Reagan in 1981. Faced with increased resistance, most unions scaled back their demands rather than risk a damaging confrontation.[15]

Indeed, after the PATCO firings, strike talk ended in the AFGE, and the postal workers voted to accept the contract they had been offered.[16] Three years later, when the next postal contract came up, the two letter carriers unions voted overwhelmingly to go to arbitration rather than strike. The *Washington Post* reported that talk at the American Postal Workers Union convention "turned frequently to the strike by air traffic controllers, 11,000 of whom were fired by President Reagan in August 1981. 'If you have an administration that would fire 11,000 highly skilled people, you know what they would do to us—fire us in a minute,' said Leland Herbert, 40, a 10-year veteran in the Los Angeles Bulk Mail Center."[17]

Nor was this effect limited to the federal level; even some mayors reported a more favorable climate for public sector union negotiations. As one union official predicted in 1981, "Now we will have thousands of little Ronald Reagans across the country in every town saying 'Fire them,' whenever public employees confronted them in a labor dispute."[18] The backlash against public sector unions spread down to state and local levels and across decades. By fall 1981, teachers unions were complaining that school boards were demanding unprecedented concessions. More than three decades after Reagan fired the PATCO strikers, Wisconsin Governor Scott Walker pushed legislation through the Wisconsin legislature to remove collective bargaining rights from most state employees. At a decisive moment in the struggle, Walker reportedly met with advisers and pulled out a picture of Ronald Reagan as inspiration.[19] All in all, labor economist Herbert R. Northrup called the PATCO strike a "watershed event" for public sector unionism in America.[20] There would be no American version of the British "winter of discontent." To the contrary, the annual number of public sector strikes and workdays lost to such strikes fell by around half in the wake of the PATCO firings; teachers' strikes in New York state fell by 90 percent and never recovered. Overall, public sector union strategy shifted away from strikes to increased political activity.[21]

Those who are committed to collective bargaining rights as a primary value are, of course, dismayed by this result of the Reagan PATCO decision. On the other hand, it seems probable that Reagan's primary accomplishment relative to public sector unions was to restore some balance that was on the verge of being lost, preventing a slippage of America into the labor chaos that afflicted pre-Thatcher Britain or that frequently plagues contemporary Italy and France. This consequence was no small thing, but it was not revolutionary, and public sector unions were far from destroyed. The percentage of public employees joining unions, which had spiked from 1960 to the mid-1970s and had al-

Table 5.1
Union members as percentage of public employees, 1949–2022

Year	Percentage Union	Year	Percentage Union
1949	12.1	1991	36.7
1953	11.6	1996	37.6
1961	10.6	2001	37.4
1966	26.1	2006	36.2
1971	33.0	2011	37.0
1976	40.2	2016	34.4
1981	35.4	2022	33.1
1986	36.0		

Source: For data 1949–2016: Julia Wolff and John Schmitt, "A Profile of Union Workers in State and Local Government," Economic Policy Institute, June 7, 2018, Figure A, https://www.epi.org/publication/a-profile-of-union-workers-in-state-and-local-government-key-facts-about-the-sector-for-followers-of-janus-v-afscme-council-31/. For data 2022: "News Release: Union Members 2022," Bureau of Labor Statistics, January 19, 2023, https://www.bls.gov/news.release/pdf/union2.pdf.

ready declined a bit from its peak, stabilized at around 35 percent, where it has remained for the last four decades (see Table 5.1). Critics today continue to complain that public sector unions hold excessive power, for example, successfully insisting that schools be shut down during the COVID pandemic despite significant negative consequences for student learning and minimal risk of transmission in the classroom.[22] If one takes seriously the cautions of Franklin Roosevelt and others about the dangers to democracy and sound government from public sector strikes, Reagan's policy of constraining PATCO was worthy of commendation rather than disdain.

Many analysts also argue that the PATCO firings contributed to the reduced power of organized labor in the private sector in the 1980s and since. In one specific respect, there is considerable evidence for this view. Reagan's strike policy made it more acceptable for businesses to hire (or threaten to hire) replacement workers. As Michael Barone noted, "Reagan's action helped to legitimize the practice of entirely destroying a union (even though PATCO broke rules which most other unions observed), and it showed workers that a union could not necessarily protect and might in fact cost them their jobs."[23] From another angle, representatives of private sector employers held that Reagan's stand reminded business that "they had the right to operate. They had the right to stay in business."[24] In the first decade after the PATCO strike, employers used permanent replacement workers in about one in seven major work stoppages; in the 1970s, the number had been about one in sixty-six.[25] Within a few years of the PATCO strike, large private firms including Greyhound, Phelps Dodge, Hormel, and International Paper had broken strikes using replacement workers.[26]

Overall, by at least three important measures, strike activity by labor unions in the United States declined dramatically after 1981, although the downward trend clearly began in the previous decade (see Table 5.2). After two decades of relative stability in all three measures—the number of major strikes, the number of workers participating in major strikes, and the days of idleness due to the strikes—the decade 1972–1981 saw a decline of 17 percent in idle days, 18 percent in major strikes, and 26 percent in workers striking. However, in the decade following the PATCO strike, strike activity further declined precipitously and has continued collapsing since then.

Thus, breaking the PATCO strike may have shifted the overall psychology of the labor-management relationship. To the extent that it reduced the power of the strike threat, it reduced the leverage of organized labor over economic outcomes in America.

Consequently, critics of Reagan contend that the decision was part of a war against labor that hurt workers across the board. Some labor economists hold that the PATCO strike significantly contributed to lower wages in later years.[27] In the words of one particularly unsubtle analyst writing in August 2021, "The murder of the U.S. middle class began 40 years ago this week."[28]

Leaving hyperbole aside, supporters of Reagan often argue that what some call a war against labor was actually a necessary effort to free the economy from the rigid grasp of organized labor, allowing the formation of a more flexible and decentralized economy capable of dynamic growth and job creation. These observers note that union demands in the 1960s

Table 5.2
Work stoppages involving 1,000 or more workers, 1952–2021

	Strikes	Number of Workers (in thousands)	Days of Idleness (in thousands)
1952–1961	3,095	14,651	244,090
1962–1971	3,091	15,394	253,523
1972–1981	2,541	11,418	209,591
1982–1991	583	4,210	85.948
1992–2001	331	2,236	56.860
2002–2011	163	946	17,184
2012–2021	148	1,027	12,921

Source: US Bureau of Labor Statistics, Annual Work Stoppages Involving 1,000 or More Workers, 1947–Present, https://www.bls.gov/web/wkstp/annual-listing.htm. Calculations by author.

and 1970s are widely blamed for declining competitiveness in fields such as automobile manufacturing and steel.[29] Indeed, an estimated 800,000 union jobs in the auto sector alone had already been lost by 1981.[30] Demands by both public and private sector employee unions may also have contributed to inflation in the 1970s, and PATCO's demands in particular threatened to set a new standard of public generosity (or profligacy) to which other public employee unions would aspire.

In this view, reducing the leverage of organized labor in the economy was a net benefit to Americans. OPM Director Donald J. Devine claimed that "Many private sector executives have told me that they were able to cut the fat from their organizations and adopt more competitive work practices because of what the government did in those days."[31] Reagan's White House Legal Counsel Peter J. Wallison argued that, with the risky step of firing the controllers, "Reagan began the process of cooling inflation psychology just as the Fed's policies were cooling the economy."[32]

Two men who bore heavy responsibility for the fight against inflation in the 1980s agree. In a 2003 speech at the Reagan Library, Federal Reserve Board chief Alan Greenspan argued that Reagan's successful fight against inflation and for deregulation had helped produce a more flexible economy.

But perhaps the most important, and then highly controversial, domestic initiative was the firing of the air traffic controllers in August

1981. The President invoked the law that striking government employees forfeit their jobs, an action that unsettled those who cynically believed no President would ever uphold that law. President Reagan prevailed, as you know, but far more importantly his action gave weight to the legal right of private employers, previously not fully exercised, to use their own discretion to both hire and discharge workers.

In Greenspan's view, this added flexibility in the labor market made it possible for the US to absorb some economic blows that would otherwise have been "debilitating."[33] Greenspan's predecessor at the Federal Reserve, Paul Volcker, likewise declared in a 2000 PBS interview that Reagan's PATCO decision was a "watershed." In Volcker's view, "One of the major factors in turning the tide on the inflationary situation was the controllers' strike" which "had a profound effect on the aggressiveness of labor at that time, in the midst of this inflationary problem and other economic problems."[34] In other words, to the extent that the breaking of the PATCO strike weakened American labor unions in general, it also contributed to the modulation of inflation, higher levels of employment and competitiveness, and relative labor peace for most of the following four decades. Critics of Reagan's strike response often do not weigh these costs and benefits side by side, or even acknowledge the tradeoffs between them—but they are inextricably linked, and the costs cannot be judged separate from the benefits.

Beyond legitimizing the use of replacement workers, the causal link between Reagan's PATCO decision and the broader fate of private sector unions is murkier. Labor arbitrator Theodore W. Kheel holds that "If PATCO was a watershed event in labor history, the strike should be viewed simply as a watershed event in the public sector."[35] For one thing, it is not clear whether the number of replacement workers hired in the 1980s actually increased; although the proportion of strikes fought with replacement workers grew, the General Accounting Office reported in the late 1980s that the overall number of replacement workers hired did not.[36] More to the point, the organizational decline of unions had begun long before 1981. Though researchers have to rely on two different sources of time-series data for this period, the best data available

Table 5.3
Union members as percentage of private sector employees, 1953–2022

Year	Percentage Union
1953	35.7
1961	31.9
1971	28.2
1981	18.7
1991	11.7
2001	9.0
2001	6.9
2022	6.0

Source: For data 1953–2011: Lawrence Mishel, Lynn Rhinehart, and Lane Windham, "Explaining the Erosion of Private-sector Unions," Economic Policy Institute, Table A, November 18, 2020, https://www.epi.org/unequalpower/publications/private-sector-unions-corporate-legal-erosion/. For data 2022: "News Release: Union Members 2022," Bureau of Labor Statistics, January 19, 2023, https://www.bls.gov/news.release/pdf/union2.pdf.

indicate that union membership peaked at just over one-third of private sector workers in 1953, then started a slow decline which picked up speed in the 1970s (see Table 5.3). By 1971, only 28.2 percent of private sector workers were union members. In 1981, the year of the PATCO strike, that number was 18.7 percent, only a little over half what it had been at its peak. Private sector union membership continued declining to 11.7 percent a decade later, before falling below one in ten, where it has remained since. In 2019, only 6.2 percent of private sector workers belonged to unions. Measured against the 1953 peak, percentage point losses in the 1970s were greater than in the 1980s.[37] Whatever the effects of Reagan's policies on organized labor, one of them was not to alter the trajectory of labor union membership in the private sector.

It is also notable that the decline of strike activity continued long after the PATCO strike was broken and long after Reagan left office. It has continued apace under presidents of both parties, including Bill Clinton and Barack Obama, both of whom filled the National Labor Relations Board with pro-union members and one of whom rescinded the

Table 5.4
Work stoppages involving 1,000 or more workers by presidential administrations

	Major Strikes	Strikes per Year
Reagan (1981–1988)	593	74.1
G. H. W. Bush (1989–1992)	170	42.5
Clinton (1993–2000)	267	33.4
G. W. Bush (2001–2008)	157	19.6
Obama (2009–2016)	117	14.6
Trump (2017–2020)	60	15.0

Source: US Bureau of Labor Statistics, Annual Work Stoppages Involving 1,000 or More Workers, 1947–Present, https://www.bls.gov/web/wkstp/annual-listing.htm. Calculations by author.

ban on FAA re-employment of the strikers. One cannot dismiss the importance of Reagan's actions against PATCO in rapidly accelerating the 1970s trend of fewer strikes, but clearly other factors are at play beyond federal labor policy, such as the pressures of international competition (see Table 5.4).

Consequently, it should not be surprising that even prolabor analyses of the decline of private sector union power in America have frequently offered explanations that do not fit neatly into the theory that Reagan's actions against PATCO bore primary or even significant responsibility for that decline. For example, three researchers from the Economic Policy Institute, a pro-union think tank, issued a report in 2020 asserting that the 1970s rather than the 1980s were the decisive decade in the downward trajectory of private sector unions. They note that in that decade, businesses became much more aggressive in using the legal tools at their disposal to fight unionization, and the number of anti-unionization consulting firms grew exponentially (from a few firms to several hundred). Even the use of replacement workers in private firms had increased substantially starting in 1975, though it "escalated" after the example set by Reagan's firing of the PATCO strikers.[38]

Kim Moody, writing for *Labor Notes*, also points the finger at the 1970s, blaming the decline of pattern bargaining for much of labor's woe, writing that:

Although most activists point to the Reagan era and the infamous firing of the PATCO air traffic controllers as the start of labor's decline, the turning point for pattern bargaining was the Chrysler bailout of 1979 and the United Auto Workers' response: accepting $203 million in givebacks. The era of concessions was on.

Membership fell, the number of strikes dropped by almost half, new organizing stalled, and the wage gains of the past were considerably trimmed if not outright reversed. None of these indicators have returned to their pre-1979 levels.[39]

Along similar lines, Steve Fraser, author of *The Age of Acquiescence*, a history of the American struggle against concentrated economic power reviewed favorably by *The Nation*, argues that the great anti-union slide began under Jimmy Carter, not Ronald Reagan.[40]

Not least, in a document entitled "The State of Our Unions" published in 2022 by the White House, President Joe Biden's Council of Economic Advisers enumerates the major causes of the long decline of private sector union membership:

> Globalization, technological change, and employer concentration are commonly cited as key factors, eroding union power and increasing employers' bargaining position relative to workers. However, many economists have pointed out that these factors do not fully explain why unionization in non-tradable sectors has fallen at a similar rate, or why unionization is lower in the United States than other Western countries. Other potential causes for declining worker power include institutional changes within the United States–particularly the breakdown of pattern bargaining in the 1980s, the expansion of right-to-work states, outsourcing and industry concentration of low-wage workers, greater employer opposition to organizing efforts, and decreased enforcement of labor laws.[41]

Neither the PATCO decision specifically nor the increased use of replacement workers more generally register on the Biden White House list.

Some analysts who are quite hostile to Reagan's labor policies acknowledge that labor had declined substantially even before Reagan's election and identify the anti-union leanings of Reagan's appointees to the National Labor Relations Board rather than PATCO as Reagan's most critical contribution to the continuation of the trends of the previous three decades. In this view, at most, Reagan may have "dealt the final blow to the New Deal system that had been under siege since 1947, when Congress passed the Taft-Hartley Act."[42] From the other side of the street, labor attorney Bernard M. Plum, who represented the Long Island Railroad in a 1989 labor dispute, holds that public attitudes toward unions had changed by 1980, so the PATCO firings "fell on fertile ground," less a cause than a result of labor's woes.[43]

Political Landscape

Aside from the widespread public approbation for his immediate response to the strike, Reagan changed the political landscape in more fundamental ways. Godfrey Hodgson argues that between the PATCO strike and Reagan's successful turning back of a railroad strike the following year, "Reagan smashed the political power the labor movement had been accumulating since the 1930s. Certainly his response to the PATCO and railroad strikes set a decisive message to union leaderships: here was a president who saw tough action against unions not as a political hazard but as a political opportunity."[44] Or, as *Detroit Free Press* labor reporter John Lippert put it, Reagan's PATCO policy "hammered home to unionists that they were no longer honored guests in the nation's corridors of power."[45] The point here is not about increased use of replacement workers or declining numbers of strikes. It is about the political power of the union movement, which had been an essential component of the Democratic Party since the New Deal. Congressional Democrats did not try to come to PATCO's rescue and were unable even to secure amnesty months or years after the firings. If organized labor was exposed as a paper tiger, so was the labor-Democratic alliance. The PATCO strike made apparent (and hence accelerated) the decline of labor's political power, and it would have done so even if there had been no subsequent additional decline of union membership.

Of course, the PATCO fight was not all gain for Reagan and Republicans. Under Reagan, as under Richard Nixon before him, some Republican strategists harbored hopes that the union movement could be politically divided. Some unions, beginning with those that had endorsed Reagan in the 1980 election, could be split off and attached permanently to a new, more blue-collar, Republican coalition. Those calculations undoubtedly played a part in Reagan's willingness to offer numerous concessions to PATCO, including salary concessions previously considered off-limits in federal contract negotiations. When an illegal strike happened anyway and Reagan fired the strikers, destroyed the union, and showed little clemency, the prospect of enticing a substantial number of unions into the new coalition was also destroyed—all the more because PATCO had joined the new coalition in 1980 but had not found protection there.

Reagan continued to appeal successfully to a large number of blue-collar voters.[46] In the 1984 election, surveys indicated that he won 58 percent of working-class voters regardless of unionization, 55 percent in households headed by an unskilled manual laborer, and 58 percent in households headed by a skilled or semiskilled manual laborer, while losing by only 47 percent to 51 percent to Walter Mondale in union families.[47] However, Republicans were unable to build structure into this coalition. Fewer unions endorsed Reagan in 1984 than in 1980; only the Teamsters remained on board. To the contrary, Reagan's PATCO stance contributed to the AFL-CIO's decision not only to remain oriented to the Democratic Party in the general election but, for the first time, to endorse a candidate for the Democratic nomination.[48] Throughout the election, from the Iowa caucuses to the November 7 general election, the unions were extraordinarily active. Of course, that labor's candidate (Mondale) won the nomination and was then badly defeated by Reagan, who won forty-nine states and 525 of 538 electoral votes, only served to accentuate the decline of labor's political power in the 1980s. But it also meant that the battle lines were clearly drawn, Republicans versus organized labor. Despite Reagan's ongoing desire to emphasize his status as a former union president, his recent PATCO-busting proved more salient to union activists and leaders than ancient history in the Screen Actors Guild.

If the PATCO firings were at cross-purposes with one of Reagan's coalitional goals, they reinforced and helped structure others, identified by political scientists Benjamin Ginsberg and Martin Shefter: to encourage blue-collar voters to make a transition in self-perception from workers to patriots, and the middle class (where American union members increasingly found themselves) from clients of government programs to taxpayers.[49] In this case, rather than identifying with PATCO as fellow unionists engaged in a tussle with The Boss, Reagan encouraged working class voters to focus on their identity as Americans. Patriotism and cultural conservatism, not labor solidarity, would be critical to their political identity. PATCO, demanding a raise larger than many blue-collar annual incomes, caricatured as a group of "bearded radicals" (in Robert Poli's words), and waging a strike that was certainly illegal and arguably endangered the safety and prosperity of the country, was a serviceable foil for this reconceptualization. Reagan did not waste time making this point; his September 3 speech in front of the United Brotherhood of Carpenters advanced these themes. He spoke to the carpenters as citizens, not workers. At the same time, opposition to the PATCO strike arguably advanced another coalitional goal of Reagan's, to reconnect small business (which feared high taxes and spending) with large business (which feared inflation and uncompetitiveness).[50]

The Republican quest to become a working-class party never disappeared. In 2022 and 2023, Democratic strategist Ruy Teixeira raised the alarm again. His party, now in thrall to white professional-class progressives, had long become inhospitable to white working-class voters and was quickly becoming that way to the nonwhite working class.[51] Republicans again had an opportunity—or perhaps it had been there all along, since George McGovern's nomination in 1972.

Some analysts also note ways that Reagan's PATCO decision advanced the philosophical underpinnings Reagan hoped to advance through his presidency. Historian Robert Dallek argues that Reagan saw the strike as an opportunity to make the point that "government and its employees would no longer exercise arbitrary control over individuals or over the course of American life."[52] To that extent, it was an important "learning moment" in Reagan's long effort to push forward a public philosophy emphasizing limited government and consent of the governed.[53] Reagan saw his job as one of building this public philosophy. This teaching moment, rather than upholding the law, was not his primary motivation when he fired the PATCO strikers, but it was nonetheless a result of his decision.

On the fortieth anniversary of the strike, Joseph A. McCartin offered another description of the ways in which the strike had altered the political landscape. Tying Reagan's PATCO response to the decline of the strike as a viable weapon of organized labor, McCartin argued that "The undermining of workers' strike power also disabled what was once a vital instrument for building and maintaining social solidarity and for directing inevitable class tensions and social conflict toward democratic and egalitarian ends." McCartin then drew a line between Reagan's strikebreaking and the January 6, 2021 insurrection, writing that "On January 6 we got a glimpse of what can grow in the vacuum created by the continued erosion of a robust tradition of workers' collective action."[54] To a degree, this interpretation is simply an acknowledgment that the aftermath of the PATCO strike inflicted long-term political damage on the left. The connection to January 6, on the other hand, would seem to require further development. As McCartin notes, the rioters were not primarily working class, leaving work to be done to identify the mechanism by which a vacuum caused by the erosion of workers' collective action was converted into a riot by middle-class Trump supporters or white supremacists. Nevertheless, McCartin's argument might point us toward a broader concern: the decline of unionization, whatever its various causes, has been a notable part of the overall deterioration of civil society which has also manifested itself in the decline of organized religion, civic groups like the Rotary and the Elks, and even intact families—deterioration which has been decried by analysts across the political spectrum as a growing danger to America's Tocquevillian democracy.[55] But this is a larger problem, not traceable to August 1981 alone.

Institutional Impact on the Presidency

There may be debate among experts over the exact character of the economic and coalitional consequences flowing from Reagan's confrontation with PATCO, but it is more clear that the PATCO strike was one of a handful of key moments defining Reagan as a strong president in the public mind. This phenomenon translated into an enhanced confidence in the presidency itself after two decades of turmoil and failure. On this point, three sets of sources agree: Reagan himself, individuals in government, and scholars and other analysts.

In his autobiography, *An American Life*, Reagan himself later called the strike his "first real national emergency." He wrote that "I didn't think of it in such terms at the time, but I suppose the strike was an important juncture for our new administration. I think it convinced people who might have thought otherwise that I meant what I said."[56]

A White House staffer at the time, Dinesh D'Souza held that the incident "set the tone for [Reagan's] presidency." In D'Souza's telling, "Reagan adopted his stern course of action without consulting pollsters, yet he was strongly supported by the country because he convinced most people that he was standing firm and upholding the law in the face of threats and intimidation. . . . Reagan proved that the right thing to do can also be politically advantageous."[57] Similarly, Edwin Harper, assistant to the president for policy development, summed it up:

> Well, one of the things that really impressed me was his courage. For example, the air traffic controllers strike: Calling their bluff on that was a real act of political courage. It took on a group that nobody had ever been willing to confront before. He did it with his eyes wide open and went ahead. It was Drew Lewis' call in some ways, but Drew Lewis was not going to do this without Ronald Reagan's permission—and I think that was a real act of political courage to do that. And it set the tone for a lot of other things.[58]

Counselor to the President Edwin Meese wrote in his memoirs that the air traffic controllers' strike was "Another crucial episode of 1981 . . . [that] reverberated both domestically *and* internationally." Meese enumerated the reasons that "the union leaders must have calculated that forceful action by the President was a remote possibility"— the long history of presidents tamely accepting illegal job actions by federal employees, the specialized training required by controllers, their importance to the functioning of commercial aviation, and PATCO's endorsement of Reagan in 1980. Yet Reagan surprised them and won the support of the American people.[59]

Writing two decades after the event, Reagan's White House Legal Counsel Peter J. Wallison connected Reagan's PATCO decision to his character as a "conviction politician" committed to principles that included the rule of law, personal responsibility, and the duty of public employees to continue doing their jobs. Many other politicians, Wallison contended, would have sought a face-saving compromising.

> But Reagan was elected as a law and order president, at a time when government at all levels seemed unable to take decisive action against powerful interests. A failure of the federal government itself to stand up to pressure—a failure simply to enforce the law against a striking union—would have undermined Reagan's effort to show that his administration would be different. . . .
>
> He could see that Americans had lost confidence in the steadfastness of their leaders and were unsure of themselves. Having been pushed around by Iranian mullahs, the Organization of Petroleum Exporting Countries (OPEC), runaway inflation, and a stagnating economy, the country could be forgiven for believing that things were out of control. Now, the air traffic controllers were threatening further havoc, attempting to extort a significantly higher wage package because of their stranglehold on the transportation economy. If Reagan was to restore the confidence of the American people, he had to show the country that someone could control events.[60]

Wallison held that two things—Reagan staying the course on his 1981 economic program and his response to the PATCO strike—"established Reagan's credibility for many of the controversies that lay ahead, substantially increasing his bargaining power with a Congress that had not recently seen a president who could not be forced into a compromise."[61] Wallison understated the degree to which Congress did sometimes force Reagan into compromises on issues including welfare reform, Social Security reform, and the large 1982 tax increase (the Tax Equity and Fiscal Responsibility Act, or TEFRA). Nevertheless, Reagan did preserve undisturbed his highest legislative priorities despite enormous pressure—the defense buildup and individual income tax rate reductions—and he won from Congress a major tax overhaul and simplification in 1986 that many observers thought impossible. On balance, there can be little doubt that the PATCO strike enhanced Reagan's credibility and that he was in a stronger political position as a result of it.

Senators with an inside view, including Senate Majority Leader Howard Baker and Reagan's friend Paul Laxalt, agreed that Reagan's stand proved crucial. Baker, for instance, contended that "It was a very decisive move. It enhanced the power of the presidency significantly at that time."[62] Similarly, in an oral history interview with the Miller Center at the University of Virginia, Laxalt later said:

> I think that established [Reagan] in the minds of an awful lot of people who aren't that political as a guy who is going to stand up and be counted. Despite all the gloomy predictions that we had—the whole system would break down, we'd have crashes everywhere—all those spots where they portrayed Reagan as an evil person....
>
> But he just developed a hell of a lot of respect for standing up and being counted, in Harry Truman style. You know what I mean? Right now, I think from that point on, the power centers in this town figured, here's a guy you better take seriously.[63]

Many outside observers—scholars and journalists—have concurred. *Washington Post* reporter Lou Cannon argued that the PATCO strike was a key moment defining Reagan as a leader: "Reagan's action sent a resonant signal of leadership that would be long remembered." In Cannon's view, "Reagan's confident decisiveness" became an important source of the public's view of his leadership and "made a good first impression on the professional politicians who dealt with him early in his presidency." Cannon also cited former (and future) Secretary of Defense Donald Rumsfeld as calling Reagan's decision "singular.... It showed his decisiveness and an ease with his instincts."[64] Haynes Johnson, writing about the Reagan years, listed PATCO as one of two events early in his presidency that turned Reagan into "a mythic figure in American life" (the other event was the assassination attempt in March 1981). In Johnson's view, Reagan's was a move of "such boldness and decisiveness" that he appeared as "the kind of leader the country longed for and thought it had lost."[65] At the time, correspondent David Broder observed, "The message is getting around. Don't mess with this guy."[66]

Scholars, as well, have consistently noted the PATCO strike as "a seminal moment that defined [Reagan's] presidency."[67] As Michael R. Adamson notes, analysts have concluded that Reagan "came off as a gutsy leader who displayed confidence and decisiveness, a man who meant what he said" (John Patrick Diggins); that he "relished the opportunity to impress Congress and the public with his decisiveness" (Michael Schaller); that Reagan "took a step that gave him an undying reputation for firmness under pressure" (James T. Patterson); and that the strike gave Reagan "another opportunity to display his resolve," through which he "instantly became a popular hero" (Sean Wilenz).[68] Biographer William E. Pemberton contended that "[Reagan's] high-profile stand ... showed him to be tough, decisive, and confident."[69] Historian Michael Beschloss likewise assessed that during the PATCO strike, Reagan "showed he was not all talk."[70] Nor was this image ephemeral. Surveying the contours of public opinion over the course of Reagan's presidency, political scientist James W. Ceaser argued that the PATCO crisis "was crucial in forming a lasting image of the President's toughness."[71]

In the terms outlined by Richard Neustadt, the PATCO strike bolstered Reagan's presidency both in terms of his professional reputation—he means what he says—and his public esteem. It was a crucial component of a first year in office that demonstrated Reagan's personal resilience (in the attempt on his life), his mastery of Congress (in passage of his tax and budget cutting program), his willingness to bloody the nose of a foreign enemy (in the fight over the Gulf of Sidra)—and, in the PATCO strike, his ability to enforce the law and keep the planes flying at the same time, a melding of principle and competence that had not been seen in the presidency for some time. One could hardly imagine a Jimmy Carter or a Gerald Ford pulling it off, and one did not need to imagine what Richard Nixon would do. In 1970, when PATCO launched a major "job action," Nixon and the FAA ultimately buckled.

Reagan's subsequent political success—his reelection with 525 electoral votes in 1984 and the election of his vice president George H. W. Bush in 1988—is thus at least partially traceable to his decisiveness against PATCO in August 1981. Hence, whatever followed from that success—from the major tax overhaul of 1986 to the modest but important start on welfare reform in 1988; from the diplomacy with Mikhail Gorbachev that ended the Cold War successfully to, on the other side of the street, the Iran-Contra affair—all are traceable to a nontrivial degree to Reagan's handling of the PATCO strike.

If Reagan's standing was boosted by the air traffic controller crisis, so was the standing of his office. Reagan's personal decisiveness translated into renewed confidence by many Americans that the presidency was a capable and potentially decisive institution.[72] When he left office, a number of analysts posited that he had, in the words of Richard Neustadt, "Restored the public image of the office to a fair (if perhaps rickety) approximation of its Rooseveltian mold: a place of popularity, influence, and initiative, a source of programmatic and symbolic leadership, both pacesetter and tonesetter, the nation's voice to both the world and us and—like or hate the policies—a presence many of us loved to see as Chief of State."[73] In the view of William E. Pemberton, Reagan "reestablished the prestige of the presidency after a string of failed administrations";[74] to political scientist Richard Nathan, the presidency had needed resuscitation, "and Ronald Reagan, in a way that surprised many observers, has accomplished precisely that."[75] With four decades of hindsight, one can see that the recovery of the presidency as an institution from its nadir in the late 1970s is traceable to Reagan's actions in 1981—and that PATCO was an important one of those actions. As Lou Cannon declared, "The one thing we know about Reagan is that he did revive confidence in the presidency."[76]

International Impact

Finally, there have been two claims advanced about the international impact of Reagan's PATCO decision. One is a claim that it influenced the labor policies of foreign governments, particularly Great Britain's. The second is that the decision had a powerful impact on how foreign economic and political leaders perceived the resolve of the American chief executive and, by extension, the United States.

On the first question, some have contended that Reagan's handling of the PATCO strike served as inspiration for Margaret Thatcher's breaking of the British coal strike in 1984–1985, but such claims are contentious. In a 1986 journal article, Teresa Ghilarducci argues that the US air traffic controllers strike "taught the Thatcher government that (as an employer) a national government could achieve broad political gains if the testing ground and forum for its policies is a dramatic confrontation with a labor union."[77] Her claim is disputed by Herbert Northrup and Duncan Campbell, who noted that Thatcher came to power in 1979 largely on the promise to stand up to unions, that she had already won enactment of three labor reform laws before the coal strike, and that her Conservative Party had already developed a strategy to privatize the coal mines in the event of labor strife the year before she took office. While Reagan and Thatcher were undoubtedly close, Northrup and Campbell argue that Thatcher hardly needed the example of PATCO to get tough with the National Union of Mineworkers.[78]

Evidence for the second claim, that Reagan's PATCO decision impacted international perceptions, is stronger. Only five days into the strike, the *Washington Post* suggested that Reagan's firmness against PATCO was "likely to reverse the dangerous erosion of presidential power at a time the Western World has maximum need for a strong presidency."[79] And indeed, just as Reagan's strike policy contributed domestically to the image of the president as a force to be reckoned with, it accomplished the same thing abroad. Scholar William Imboden addresses the PATCO controversy in his 2022 book *The Peacemaker: Ronald Reagan, the Cold War, and the World on the Brink*, a comprehensive examination of Reagan's foreign policy. Imboden observes that "The PATCO strike may have appeared at first only a domestic issue, but it quickly became international. . . . World leaders watched to see how this new president would handle the crisis." When Reagan held firm, "Many around the world took notice."[80]

Columnist Haynes Johnson pointed to international financiers who frequently claimed that their confidence in Reagan's seriousness about controlling inflation dated from "when Reagan broke the controllers' strike."[81] More crucially, according to several sources, Soviet leaders took lessons from Reagan's response to the strike. The White House first realized that the Kremlin was paying attention when the Soviet news agency TASS condemned Reagan's "brutal repression" of the strikers.[82] Noted Sovietologist Richard Pipes said "The way the PATCO strike was handled impressed the Russians . . . and gave them respect for Reagan.

It showed them a man who, when aroused, will go to the limit to back up his principles."[83] Pipes conveyed that Soviet leaders were particularly struck by pictures in the media of PATCO official Steven L. Wallaert in manacles after his August 5 arrest. After a business trip to Moscow, Archer Daniels Midland CEO Dwayne Andreas privately reported to House Speaker Tip O'Neill "that the Soviet top brass had shared with him their healthy respect for the new president. The Russians, he said, credited Reagan, in contrast to his predecessors, with the strength of will to qualify him as a true leader."[84] Reagan advisers who counselled against rehiring the PATCO strikers because such a course might send mixed signals to foreign governments that had heretofore been "very impressed with the President's strong position on the issue" were most concerned with Soviet perceptions. According to the argument, which prevailed with Reagan, "By showing that he would carry through on his threats and defend his principles no matter the cost and despite critics who called for a softer approach, Reagan could reinforce his image of toughness.... The more costly the strike, and the more his refusal to rehire strikers was perceived as stubborn or even risky, the more his image as a strong world leader would benefit from it."[85] Reagan's initial decision to fire the strikers made a big impression, which was preserved intact by his subsequent decision not to rehire them.

For this reason, Reagan's first national security adviser, Richard V. Allen, called the firing of the PATCO strikers "Reagan's first foreign policy decision."[86] George Shultz, who served Reagan as secretary of state from 1982 through the end of his presidency, said that "The world learned when Ronald Reagan faced down the air-traffic controllers in 1981 that he could dig in and fight to win."[87] Reagan speechwriter Peggy Noonan relates that Shultz once remarked that the firing of the strikers was the most important foreign policy decision Reagan made.[88] This was an astounding statement. Shultz had, after all, witnessed Reagan's decisions to invade Grenada, introduce Marines into Lebanon (and then withdraw them), install Pershing II and cruise missiles in Europe over the objections of the antinuclear movement, push for the Strategic Defense Initiative, hold multiple summit meetings with Mikhail Gorbachev, sign the Intermediate Nuclear Forces Treaty eliminating a class of nuclear weapons, step up aid to anti-Communist guerrillas in third world countries, bomb Libya, and (against Shultz's advice) secretly sell arms to Iran. Thus, early in Reagan's presidency, the PATCO crisis set a tone that told foreign adversaries: This is not a man who bluffs or who can be rolled. As his biographer Edmund Morris contended, Reagan was "a sheriff who was capable of swift hard action."[89]

In the turbulent 1980s, in a world filled with well-armed and malevolent adversaries, that impression may have been the single most important prerequisite for the preservation of peace. Hence, of all the consequences of Reagan's PATCO decision, this one may have been the most significant. Former CIA analyst Herbert E. Meyer contends that at the beginning of the 1980s, the Soviet leadership realized that the West was beginning to open up a major technological advantage over them. This meant that their window of opportunity for expansionism was closing. At that point, the Soviets had two choices: "Change, or get through that window before it comes down on you."[90] Had they doubted the steadfastness of the president of the United States, catastrophe might easily have ensued.

Conclusion

Ronald Reagan entered office in January 1981, having been endorsed by the Professional Air Traffic Controllers Organization and having expressed sympathy for the controllers' plight. Seven months later, confronted by an illegal strike and union demands that in his view threatened to explode the federal budget, Reagan made the difficult decision to fire the strikers, prosecute their leaders, and decertify their union. Once the decision was made, he never wavered.

Although Reagan himself held that the law left him no choice, he took a very different approach than that taken by his predecessors, who had accommodated previous illegal PATCO actions. This moment revealed early in Reagan's presidency two important features of his political style. First, it served as an example of his management approach at its best. He afforded a general direction to subordinates, delegated much to them, then was prepared to render a decisive judgment if circumstances forced the issue up to his level. As his Attorney General William French Smith later wrote, in the PATCO situation (and in similar cases), "It was Ronald Reagan who knew what the decision had to be, and he directed its implementation. Such decisions were his decisions, and came from deep within him." Reagan was, according to Smith, "hands-on all the way" in this instance.[1]

Second, the episode illuminated Reagan's ability to use the material at hand to fashion a public lesson that brought "learning" which far exceeded the immediate importance of the decision. He was able, in other words, to leverage a decision of moderate immediate importance—an action against a belligerent but fundamentally overextended foe—into a lesson of much greater import. The PATCO strike furnished a pattern. The 1981 duel with Libyan fighter jets over the Gulf of Sidra was another such moment; the 1983 invasion of Grenada yet another; the bombing of Qaddafi in April 1986 a fourth. As Michael Barone argues, the PATCO decision "had an effect far out of proportion to the number of people directly affected."[2]

In retrospect, as with most of Reagan's important actions, this decision was telegraphed months or even years in advance for those willing to see. Reagan was a conviction politician, as his White House Legal Counsel Peter Wallison notes, and by 1981 his convictions were well established. If his opposition to public employee strikes as Governor of California or his 1977 syndicated radio broadcast on the subject were not sufficient to foretell his position on the PATCO strike, his repeated declarations as president, up through August 2, certainly did. Through Drew Lewis, Reagan conveyed to both the union and the public that a strike would not be tolerated.

While the short-term consequences of the PATCO firings were not trivial, it was the long-term consequences that make it a presidential decision of real significance. As Peggy Noonan put it: "Everyone knew [the PATCO strike] was important, but no one knew how important. And everyone knew it was a domestic crisis, but no one knew it was a foreign affairs triumph."[3] The consequences were wide-ranging. Reagan did not alter the long downward trajectory of private sector union membership, but his response to PATCO accelerated the use of permanent replacement workers by employers and the decline of the strike, undermining the influence of unions over economic life for better and worse. Critics blame the decision for lower wages and loss of social solidarity, while Reagan's supporters argue that it helped forge a more flexible economy that defeated inflation and maintained higher employment than the more rigid labor markets of the European social democracies. Meanwhile, long-term political coalitions were impacted, the trajectory of public sector unions was stabilized, and Reagan's political prestige— and with it, the prestige of the presidency as an institution—was burnished. And abroad, in a world where the aggressive aspirations of a totalitarian empire remained the preeminent threat to peace, Reagan's decision provided some much-needed clarity. This president would stand his ground.

It is notable just how often observers have used superlatives when discussing these consequences. Reagan's response to the PATCO strike has been described variously as "a watershed event" and "pivotal" for public sector unionism, for overall labor-management relations, or for the economy generally (Herbert R. Northrup, Theodore W. Kheel, Willis J. Nordlund, Paul Volcker, Millie Allen Beik);[4] "a game-changing event in American industrial relations" (Joseph A. McCartin);[5] "perhaps the most important" domestic initiative Reagan took (Alan Greenspan);[6] "crucial in forming a lasting image of the President's toughness" (James W. Ceaser);[7] the most important foreign policy decision Reagan made (George Shultz);[8] and "one of the most important actions [Reagan] took in his entire two terms" (William Krupman).[9]

Two ironies attended these consequences, however one assesses them. The first is that they were as dependent on PATCO as on Reagan. Had the union accepted the June 22 contract, which had been endorsed by Reagan and signed off on by Drew Lewis, none of them would have happened. PATCO would have survived, its members would have taken home salary and hours concessions, and the chief story would have been how far Reagan and his administration had bent in order to preserve labor peace (and help out a political ally). Only the decision by the union to strike crossed Reagan's red line and triggered his determined response.

The second irony is that, as important as the economic, political, institutional, and international consequences were, they did not represent Reagan's driving, central goal. He was certainly aware of the possible negative implications on the federal budget, on the fight against inflation, and on perceptions of his steadfastness at home and abroad if he were to give in. His advisers were even more attuned to those considerations. And there can be little doubt that both Reagan and his advisers were well-pleased with most of the long-term consequences that issued from the decision. But, to Reagan, these were incidental benefits. His public statements, his private discussions with advisers, and even his diary entries consistently indicated that his driving consideration was simply, in accordance with his constitutional obligation, to "Take care that the law be faithfully executed."

What broader lessons are illustrated by the PATCO strike and Reagan's response? One is the power of miscalculation. PATCO plunged ahead with its doomed strike not only because air controllers harbored two decades of grievances and resentment toward the FAA, but because the union miscalculated almost everything: Reagan's intentions and level of determination, to be sure, but also the efficacy of the FAA contingency plan, support for the union in Congress, in the airlines, and in other unions, the ability of foreign unions to bring transatlantic flights to a halt, the likelihood of federal judges enforcing the standing injunction, and the importance of public opinion to their struggle. Reagan, too, may have miscalculated the militancy of the union and the percentage of PATCO members who would stay on strike despite the forty-eight-hour deadline, but he and Drew Lewis provided many clear warnings. A related point is that unexamined assumptions can be dangerous: At a critical juncture, PATCO's endorsement of Reagan may have made it harder for him to compromise; and rather than making PATCO invincible, its apparent stranglehold over the economy may have made Americans more willing to see Reagan break the strike.

Another broad lesson is the power of a president taking a stand on the basis of genuinely held beliefs. There were certainly practical arguments that contributed to public support for Reagan, but the practical arguments were always married to moral arguments. It is not right to take an oath not to strike and then go on strike. It is not right to break the law. It is not right to take a job that is responsible for the safety of thousands of people every day and then walk off that job. For that matter, it is not right to demand that government tax the people to increase your already-high salary when everyone else is tightening their belts. These were Reagan's moral arguments, and the public sensed that Reagan deeply believed them. The fact that PATCO had no good answer effectively neutralized congressional Democrats, the liberal media, and the labor movement. Soon after the strike began, the *Washington Post* correctly perceived that "Reagan's sense of his own rectitude is the real guarantee against retreat."[10]

A third lesson is the importance and utility of combining tactical flexibility and strategic constancy. Reagan wanted a reasonable deal if he could get one. If he could not, he wanted to uphold the no-strike law. In pursuit of the former, he allowed Drew Lewis flexibility to negotiate. When PATCO struck, he offered a forty-eight-hour window for the strikers to return. Once the deadline arrived, he was resolute, and there would be no negotiation or amnesty. When public opinion and the media took a turn toward clemency, he conceded just enough to satisfy the public while fundamentally retaining the core of his position.

Fourth, the PATCO controversy reminds us that no presidential decision takes place in a vacuum. If the president wants to be successful, it helps for the broader political environment to be favorable. In this case, it was. Congress had just passed Reagan's economic program, the public was giving Reagan high marks while declaring inflation its number one concern, and even politics at the state level had seen a turn against spending and high taxes. Once the strike began, the coordinate branches lined up against it, as did most of the media; business backed the president, while labor was ambivalent; and public opinion polls approved the president's response by a two-to-one margin. Reagan's policy was not driven by public opinion, but was affirmed by it, an outcome he may well have anticipated. From his days on the General Electric speaking circuit to his travels around California preparing for his 1966 gubernatorial campaign to his subsequent presidential campaigns, Reagan learned much from his audiences. In the process, he developed a generally reliable sense of the values and priorities of a wide slice of the American people. He brought that sense to the PATCO crisis.

Finally, Reagan's decision was taken at considerable risk, enough so that some critics saw it as reckless. The economic and human costs in the short term could have been much higher. That the contingency plan generally worked and there was no "aluminum rain" was, to some extent, a matter of good fortune (or, Reagan might have said, Providence). But it was also the result of considerable preparation, including rigorous updating and bolstering of the contingency plan that had been inherited from the Carter FAA, a process that started shortly after his inauguration and accelerated after the June 22 strike scare. The payoff for the risk was great, up to and including reduction of the danger of nuclear war. There may have been presidents in American history who would have taken the dramatic decision but without the preparation; there are certainly some who would not have taken the risk, no matter the preparation. It is doubtful that either alternative would have served the country better.

Famously, the ancient Romans declared that "Fortune favors the brave." An alternative version, less well-known but no less relevant, proclaimed that "Fortune favors the prepared mind." In August 1981, Reagan taught the lesson that presidents are well-advised to seek fortune from both sources.

APPENDIX A

Timeline: Ronald Reagan and the PATCO Strike

1977

May 25: Reagan delivers syndicated radio commentary entitled "Public Servants," criticizing public employee strikes.

1980

October 20: Reagan signs letter to PATCO promising to do "whatever necessary" to improve air traffic control.

October 23: PATCO President Robert E. Poli meets with Reagan and says he is impressed; PATCO endorses Reagan for president.

November 4: Reagan defeats Jimmy Carter in US presidential election.

1981

January 20: Reagan inaugurated fortieth president of the United States.

February 3: Congressman Clay introduces H.R. 1576 based on PATCO's key negotiating goals.

February 10: Reagan meets with Poli and other labor leaders in the White House.

February 12: PATCO/FAA contract negotiations begin.

March 30: John Hinckley Jr. shoots and seriously wounds Reagan outside the Washington Hilton.

April 28: Poli walks out of negotiations.

April 30: At congressional hearings, Transportation Secretary Drew Lewis is conciliatory but also warns PATCO against an illegal strike; Poli vows "no strike" but implicitly threatens one.

May 22: At PATCO convention, PATCO board announces possible strike date of June 22.

June 11: Drew Lewis proposes a deal including increased pay, reduced work hours, and other items totaling $40 million; at a meeting, Meese, Stockman, and others agree.

June 12: Reagan approves the Lewis offer.

June 17: PATCO returns to talks; Drew Lewis represents FAA in person.

June 18: Federal Judge Thomas C. Platt refuses PATCO's request to vacate the 1970 injunction against a PATCO strike.

June 20: Reagan orders the Justice Department to prepare to seek injunctions against a PATCO strike.

June 22: Poli and Lewis come to terms on a tentative contract after Poli learns that PATCO membership vote fell short of the 80 percent support the union had declared as the threshold for a strike. Poli refers to the contract as "fair."

July 2: PATCO board votes nine to zero to recommend rejection of the contract; Poli is one of the nine.

July 30: PATCO membership rejects the proposed contract with a 95 percent "no" vote.

July 31: Lewis requests more flexibility in negotiations from White House and asks Poli for seven more days of negotiation. Poli rejects, sets August 3 strike date. Reagan's tax cut bill passes both houses of Congress.

August 2: Lewis offers to let PATCO allocate the $40 million package as it wanted and warns Poli there will be no negotiations and no amnesty if PATCO goes on strike.

August 3: PATCO strike begins; Reagan meets with advisers and finalizes decision to set a forty-eight-hour deadline for strikers to return before being fired. At around 11 a.m. eastern time, Reagan makes a statement and announces the deadline. Also:

- FAA contingency plan goes into effect.
- Administration requests decertification of PATCO by the Federal Labor Relations Authority.

- Federal Judges Harold H. Greene in Washington, DC and Thomas C. Platt in New York declare PATCO in contempt and impose large fines and damages.
- Federal arrest and prosecution of strike leaders begins; ultimately seventy-eight are prosecuted.

August 5: Reagan reaffirms decision to fire strikers; Lewis declares strike over and issues dismissal letters.

August 6–7: First major public opinion surveys show the public supporting Reagan's decision to fire the strikers by roughly a two-to-one margin.

August 13: Reagan signs budget and tax cut legislation at his California ranch; Reagan reaffirms controllers decision again and says no amnesty.

August 14: Administrative Law Judge John Fenton recommends that the Federal Labor Relations Authority take measures to decertify PATCO.

August 19: US Navy F-14s shoot down two Libyan fighter planes that had fired on them in the Gulf of Sidra.

August 26: Word comes down from Meese to administration officials that there is to be no further discussions, even informal, related to amnesty for fired strikers.

September 3: Reagan speaks at convention of United Brotherhood of Carpenters and reiterates his position.

September 19: AFL-CIO Solidarity Day labor march and rally in Washington, DC; approximately 250,000 attend.

October 22: Federal Labor Relations Authority votes two to one to decertify PATCO.

November 3: Decertification goes into effect.

December 1: Reagan suggests the possibility of allowing fired PATCO strikers to apply for federal employment, though not as controllers.

December 2: Reagan meets with AFL-CIO executive council at the White House, hears pleas to return strikers to work; again floats possibility of allowing them to apply for federal jobs outside the FAA.

December 7: Office of Personnel Management Direct Dan Devine writes a memo advocating the policy Reagan had suggested on December 1 and 2 as the best possible choice.

December 9: At a meeting with key advisers including Drew Lewis and the Troika, Reagan accepts Devine's proposal; announces change in policy.

December 31: Robert E. Poli and Robert Meyer resign as president and vice-president of PATCO.

1982

January 1: Gary Eads becomes president of PATCO.

June 11: PATCO loses its appeal of decertification in federal court.

June 25: PATCO board votes to dissolve PATCO and declare bankruptcy.

APPENDIX B

Ronald Reagan Letter to Robert E. Poli, President of the Professional Air Traffic Controllers Organization, October 20, 1981

Dear Mr. Poli,

I have been thoroughly briefed by members of my staff as to the deplorable state of our nation's air traffic control system. They have told me that too few people working unreasonable hours with obsolete equipment has placed the nation's air travellers in unwarranted danger.

In an area so clearly related to public safety, the Carter Administration has failed to act responsibly.

You can rest assured that if I am elected president, I will take whatever steps necessary to provide our air traffic controllers with the most modern equipment available and to adjust staff levels and work days so that they are commensurate with achieving a maximum degree of public safety.

As in all other areas of the federal government where the president has power of appointment, I fully intend to appoint highly qualified individuals who can work harmoniously with the Congress and the employees of the government agencies they oversee.

I pledge to you that my administration will work very closely with you to bring about a spirit of cooperation between the president and the air traffic controllers. Such harmony can and must exist if we are to restore the people's confidence in their government.

Sincerely,
Ronald Reagan

Source: Arthur B. Shostak and David Skocik, *The Air Controllers' Controversy: Lessons from the PATCO Strike* (New York: Authors Choice, 2006), 80.

APPENDIX C

Transcript of Reagan Remarks and Question-and-Answer Session with Reporters on the Air Traffic Controllers Strike, August 3, 1981

THE PRESIDENT. This morning at 7 a.m. the union representing those who man America's air traffic control facilities called a strike. This was the culmination of 7 months of negotiations between the Federal Aviation Administration and the union. At one point in these negotiations agreement was reached and signed by both sides, granting a $40 million increase in salaries and benefits. This is twice what other government employees can expect. It was granted in recognition of the difficulties inherent in the work these people perform. Now, however, the union demands are 17 times what had been agreed to—$681 million. This would impose a tax burden on their fellow citizens which is unacceptable.

I would like to thank the supervisors and controllers who are on the job today, helping to get the nation's air system operating safely. In the New York area, for example, four supervisors were scheduled to report for work, and 17 additionally volunteered. At National Airport a traffic controller told a newsperson he had resigned from the union and reported to work because, "How can I ask my kids to obey the law if I don't?" This is a great tribute to America.

Let me make one thing plain. I respect the right of workers in the private sector to strike. Indeed, as president of my own union, I led the first strike ever called by that union. I guess I'm maybe the first one to ever hold this office who is a lifetime member of an AFL-CIO union. But we cannot compare labor-management relations in the private sector with government. Government cannot close down the assembly line. It has to provide without interruption the protective services which are government's reason for being.

It was in recognition of this that the Congress passed a law forbidding strikes by government employees against the public safety. Let me read the solemn oath taken by each of these employees, a sworn affidavit, when they accepted their jobs: "I am not participating in any strike against the Government of the United States or any agency thereof, and I will not so participate while an employee of the Government of the United States or any agency thereof."

It is for this reason that I must tell those who fail to report for duty this morning they are in violation of the law, and if they do not report for work within 48 hours, they have forfeited their jobs and will be terminated.

Q. Mr. President, are you going to order any union members who violate the law to go to jail?

THE PRESIDENT. Well, I have some people around here, and maybe I should refer that question to the Attorney General.

Q. Do you think that they should go to jail, Mr. President, anybody who violates this law?

THE PRESIDENT. I told you what I think should be done. They're terminated.

THE ATTORNEY GENERAL. Well, as the President has said, striking under these circumstances constitutes a violation of the law, and we intend to initiate in appropriate cases criminal proceedings against those who have violated the law.

Q. How quickly will you initiate criminal proceedings, Mr. Attorney General?

THE ATTORNEY GENERAL. We will initiate those proceedings as soon as we can.

Q. Today?

THE ATTORNEY GENERAL. The process will be underway probably by noon today.

Q. Are you going to try and fine the union $1 million per day?

THE ATTORNEY GENERAL. Well, that's the prerogative of the court. In the event that any individuals are found guilty of contempt of a court order, the penalty for that, of course, is imposed by the court.

Q. How much more is the government prepared to offer the union?

THE SECRETARY OF TRANSPORTATION. We think we had a very satisfactory offer on the table. It's twice what other Government employees are going to get—11.4 percent. Their demands were so unreasonable there was no spot to negotiate, when you're talking to somebody 17 times away from where you presently are. We do not plan to increase our offer to the union.

Q. Under no circumstances?

THE SECRETARY OF TRANSPORTATION. As far as I'm concerned, under no circumstance.

Q. Will you continue to meet with them?

THE SECRETARY OF TRANSPORTATION. We will not meet with the union as long as they're on strike. When they're off of strike, and assuming that they are not decertified, we will meet with the union and try to negotiate a satisfactory contract.

Q. Do you have any idea how it's going at the airports around the country?

THE SECRETARY OF TRANSPORTATION. Relatively, it's going quite well. We're operating somewhat in excess of 50 percent capacity. We could increase that. We have determined, until we feel we're in total control of the system, that we will not increase that. Also, as you probably know, we have some rather severe weather in the Midwest, and our first priority is safety.

Q. What can you tell us about possible decertification of the union and impoundment of its strike funds?

THE SECRETARY OF TRANSPORTATION. There has been a court action to impound the strike fund of $3.5 million. We are going before the National Labor Relations Authority this morning and ask for decertification of the union.

Q. When you say that you're not going to increase your offer, are you referring to the original offer or the last offer which you've made? Is that still valid?

THE SECRETARY OF TRANSPORTATION. The last offer we made in present value was exactly the same as the first offer. Mr. Poli asked me about 11 o'clock last evening if he could phase the increase in over a period of time. For that reason, we phased it in over a longer period of time. It would have given him a larger increase in terms of where he would be when the next negotiations started, but in present value it was the $40 million originally on the table.

Q. Mr. Attorney General, in seeking criminal action against the union leaders, will you seek to put them in jail if they do not order these people back to work?

THE ATTORNEY GENERAL. Well, we will seek whatever penalty is appropriate under the circumstances in each individual case.

Q. Do you think that is an appropriate circumstance?

THE ATTORNEY GENERAL. It is certainly one of the penalties that is provided for in the law, and in appropriate cases, we could very well seek that penalty.

Q. What's appropriate?

THE ATTORNEY GENERAL. Well, that depends upon the fact of each case.

Q. What makes the difference?

Q. Can I go back to my "fine" question? How much would you like to see the union fined every day?

THE ATTORNEY GENERAL. Well, there's no way to answer that question.

We would just have to wait until we get into court, see what the circumstances are, and determine what position we would take in the various cases under the facts as they develop.

Q. But you won't go to court and ask the court for a specific amount?

THE ATTORNEY GENERAL. Well, I'm sure we will when we reach that point, but there's no way to pick a figure now.

Q. Mr. President, will you delay your trip to California or cancel it if the strike is still on later this week?

THE PRESIDENT. If any situation should arise that would require my presence here, naturally I will do that. So, that will be a decision that awaits what's going to happen. May I just—because I have to be back in there for another appointment—may I just say one thing on top of this? With all this talk of penalties and everything else, I hope that you'll emphasize, again, the possibility of termination, because I believe that there are a great many of those people—and they're fine people—who have been swept up in this and probably have not really considered the result—the fact that they had taken an oath, the fact that this is now in violation of the law, as that one supervisor referred to with regard to his children. And I am hoping that they will in a sense remove themselves from the lawbreaker situation by returning to their posts.

I have no way to know whether this had been conveyed to them by their union leaders, who had been informed that this would be the result of a strike.

Q. Your deadline is 7 o'clock Wednesday morning for them to return to work?

THE PRESIDENT. Forty-eight hours.

THE SECRETARY OF TRANSPORTATION. It's 11 o'clock Wednesday morning.

Q. Mr. President, why have you taken such strong action as your first action? Why not some lesser action at this point?

THE PRESIDENT. What lesser action can there be? The law is very explicit. They are violating the law. And as I say, we called this to the attention of their leadership. Whether this was conveyed to the membership before they voted to strike, I don't know. But this is one of the reasons why there can be no further negotiation while this situation continues. You can't sit and negotiate with a union that's in violation of the law.

THE SECRETARY OF TRANSPORTATION. And their oath.

THE PRESIDENT. And their oath.

Q. Are you more likely to proceed in the criminal direction toward the leadership than the rank and file, Mr. President?

THE PRESIDENT. Well, that again is not for me to answer.

Q. Mr. Secretary, what can you tell us about the possible use of military air controllers—how many, how quickly can they get on the job?

THE SECRETARY OF TRANSPORTATION. In answer to the previous question, we will move both civil and criminal, probably more civil than criminal, and we now have papers in the U.S. attorneys' offices, under the Attorney General, in about 20 locations around the country where would be involved two or three principal people. As far as the military personnel are concerned, they are going to fundamentally be backup to the supervisory personnel. We had 150 on the job, supposedly, about a half-hour ago. We're going to increase that to somewhere between 700 and 850.

Q. Mr. Secretary, are you ready to hire other people should these other people not return?

THE SECRETARY OF TRANSPORTATION. Yes, we will, and we hope we do not reach that point. Again as the President said, we're hoping these people come back to work. They do a fine job. If that does not take place, we have a training school, as you know. We will be advertising. We have a number of applicants right now. There's a waiting list in terms of people that want to be controllers, and we'll start retraining and reorganize the entire FAA traffic controller group.

Q. Just to clarify, is your deadline 7 a.m. Wednesday or 11 o'clock?

THE SECRETARY OF TRANSPORTATION. It's 11 a.m. Wednesday. The President said 48 hours, and that would be 48 hours.

Q. If you actually fire these people, won't it put your air traffic control system in a hole for years to come, since you can't just cook up a controller in—[inaudible]?

THE SECRETARY OF TRANSPORTATION. That obviously depends on how many return to work. Right now we're able to operate the system. In some areas, we've been very gratified by the support we've received. In other areas, we've been disappointed. And until I see the numbers, there's no way I can answer that question.

Q. Mr. Lewis, did you tell the union leadership when you were talking to them that their members would be fired if they went out on strike?

THE SECRETARY OF TRANSPORTATION. I told Mr. Poll [*sic*] yesterday that the President gave me three instructions in terms of the firmness of the negotiations: one is there would be no amnesty; the second there would be no negotiations during the strike; and third is that if they went on strike, these people would no longer be government employees.

Q. Mr. Secretary, you said no negotiations. What about informal meetings of any kind with Mr. Poli?

THE SECRETARY OF TRANSPORTATION. We will have no meetings until the strike is terminated with the union.

Q. Have you served Poli at this point? Has he been served by the Attorney General?

THE ATTORNEY GENERAL. In the civil action that was filed this morning, the service was made on the attorney for the union, and the court has determined that that was appropriate service on all of the officers of the union.

Q. My previous question about whether you're going to take a harder line on the leadership than rank and file in terms of any criminal prosecution, can you give us an answer on that?

THE ATTORNEY GENERAL. No, I can't answer that except to say that each case will be investigated on its own merits, and action will be taken as appropriate in each of those cases.

Q. Mr. Lewis, do you know how many applications for controller jobs you have on file now?

THE SECRETARY OF TRANSPORTATION. I do not know. I'm going to check when I get back. I am aware there's a waiting list, and I do not have the figure. If you care to have that, you can call our office, and we'll tell you. Also, we'll be advertising and recruiting people for this job if necessary.

Q. Mr. Secretary, how long are you prepared to hold out if there's a partial but not complete strike?

THE SECRETARY OF TRANSPORTATION. I think the President made it very clear that as of 48 hours from now, if the people are not back on the job, they will not be government employees at any time in the future.

Q. How long are you prepared to run the air controller system—[inaudible]?

THE SECRETARY OF TRANSPORTATION. For years, if we have to.

Q. How long does it take to train a new controller, from the waiting list?

THE SECRETARY OF TRANSPORTATION. It varies; it depends on the type of center they're going to be in. For someone to start in the system and work through the more minor office types of control situations till they get to, let's say, a Chicago or a Washington National, it takes about 3 years. So in this case, what we'll have to do if some of the major metropolitan areas are shut down or a considerable portion is shut down, we'll be bringing people in from other areas that are qualified and then start bringing people through the training schools in the smaller cities and smaller airports.

Q. Mr. Secretary, have you definitely made your final offer to the union?

THE SECRETARY OF TRANSPORTATION. Yes, we have.

Q. Thank you.

Source: Ronald Reagan, Remarks and a Question-and-Answer Session with Reporters on the Air Traffic Controllers Strike, online by Gerhard Peters and John T. Woolley, The American Presidency Project, https://www.presidency.ucsb.edu/node/246781.

NOTES

CHAPTER 1. THE SETTING

1. Herbert Northrup, "The Rise and Demise of PATCO," *Industrial and Labor Relations Review* 37, no. 2 (January 1984): 167–184.
2. Rebecca Pels, "The Pressures of PATCO: Strikes and Stress in the 1980s," *Essays in History* 37 (1995): 1–18.
3. Willis J. Nordlund, *Silent Skies: The Air Traffic Controllers' Strike* (Westport, CT: Praeger, 1998), 193.
4. Ronald Reagan, *An American Life: The Autobiography* (New York: Simon and Schuster, 1990), 114. Reagan's account of his time in the Screen Actors Guild more generally can be found on 89–90, 103, 107–109, 113, 114, 118.
5. Edward M. Yager, *Ronald Reagan's Journey: Democrat to Republican* (Lanham, MD: Rowman & Littlefield, 2006).
6. Joseph A. McCartin, *Collision Course: Ronald Reagan, the Air Traffic Controllers, and the Strike that Changed America* (New York: Oxford University Press, 2011), 243–245; "Memorandum for David Gergen from Ed Gray," Gergen, PATCO file. McCartin's account emphasizes Reagan's flexibility; the internal Reagan Administration memorandum from Gray to Gergen emphasizes his firmness.
7. Kiron K. Skinner, Annelise Anderson, and Martin Anderson, eds., *Reagan in His Own Hand: The Writings of Ronald Reagan that Reveal His Revolutionary Vision for America* (New York: Free Press, 2001), 300.
8. Andrew E. Busch, *Reagan's Victory: The Election of 1980 and the Rise of the Right* (Lawrence: University Press of Kansas, 2005).
9. Busch, *Reagan's Victory*, 127.
10. Richard Harwood, ed., *The Pursuit of the Presidency 1980* (New York: Berkeley Books, 1980), cover.
11. Theodore White, *America in Search of Itself: The Making of the President 1956–1980* (New York: Warner Books, 1982).
12. Forty percent of Reagan voters declared inflation and economy one of their top two issues, followed by 26 percent who said a balanced budget and 20 percent who named jobs and unemployment. Douglas A. Hibbs, Jr., "President Reagan's Mandate from the 1980 Election: A Shift to the Right?," *American Politics Quarterly* 10 (October 1982): 387–420.
13. Office of Management and Budget, Budget of the United States Historical Tables, Tables 1.3 and 3.1, https://www.whitehouse.gov/omb/budget/historical-tables/.
14. Martin Anderson, *Revolution* (New York: Harcourt Brace Jovanovich, 1988), 138.
15. Ben Wattenberg, "It's Time to Stop America's Retreat," *New York Times Magazine*, July 22, 1979.

16. McCartin, *Collision Course*, 316.

17. See, for example, Lloyd N. Cutler, "To Form a Government," *Foreign Affairs* 59, no. 1 (Fall 1980): 126–143.

18. Richard Neustadt, *Presidential Power: The Politics of Leadership from FDR to Carter*, 3rd ed. (New York: Wiley, 1980), 208.

19. Sidney M. Milkis and Michael Nelson, *The American Presidency: Origins and Development, 1776–1990* (Washington, DC: CQ, 1990), 333.

20. Richard Neustadt, *Presidential Power and the Modern Presidents* (New York: Free Press, 1990), esp. 10–90.

21. Ronald Reagan, Inaugural Address Online by Gerhard Peters and John T. Woolley, The American Presidency Project, https://www.presidency.ucsb.edu/node/246336.

22. For detailed reviews of the battles by two insiders, see Anderson, *Revolution*, and David Stockman, *The Triumph of Politics: Why the Reagan Revolution Failed* (New York: Harper & Row, 1986).

23. Samuel Kernell, *Going Public* (Washington, DC: CQ, 2006).

24. Reagan, *An American Life*, 284–288.

25. Jacob Weisberg, *Ronald Reagan* (New York: Times Books, 2016), 71–73; Edmund Morris, *Dutch: A Memoir of Ronald Reagan* (New York: Random House, 1999), 447–452.

26. Bernard D. Meltzer and Cass R. Sunstein, "Public Employee Strikes, Executive Discretion, and the Air Traffic Controllers," *The University of Chicago Law Review* 50, no. 2 (Spring 1983): 736.

27. Daniel DiSalvo, *Government Against Itself: Public Union Power and Its Consequences* (New York: Oxford University Press, 2015), 1.

28. DiSalvo, *Government Against Itself*, 195.

29. DiSalvo, *Government Against Itself*, 49.

30. McCartin, *Collision Course*, 9.

31. Julia Wolff and John Schmitt, "A Profile of Union Workers in State and Local Government," Economic Policy Institute, June 7, 2018, Figure A, https://www.epi.org/publication/a-profile-of-union-workers-in-state-and-local-government-key-facts-about-the-sector-for-followers-of-janus-v-afscme-council-31/.

32. Meltzer and Sunstein, "Public Employee Strikes, Executive Discretion, and the Air Traffic Controllers," 735–746.

33. McCartin, *Collision Course*, 16–17.

34. The summary account of the creation and development of PATCO found over the next several pages draws heavily from McCartin, *Collision Course*, ch. 1-8; see also Willis J. Nordlund, *Silent Skies: The Air Traffic Controllers' Strike* (Westport, CT: Praeger, 1998), ch. 3; Arthur B. Shostak and David Skocik, *The Air Controllers' Controversy: Lessons from the PATCO Strike* (New York: Authors Choice, 2006), ch. 3-5; Northrup, "The Rise and Demise of PATCO."

35. McCartin, *Collision Course*, 135–143.

36. McCartin, *Collision Course*, 145.

37. McCartin, *Collision Course*, 225. Poli continued using the phrase after be-

coming president of PATCO, even as negotiations with the FAA approached a critical point in 1981; Nordlund, *Silent Skies*, 90.

38. Meltzer and Sunstein, "Public Employee Strikes, Executive Discretion, and the Air Traffic Controllers," 765.

39. Meltzer and Sunstein, "Public Employee Strikes, Executive Discretion, and the Air Traffic Controllers," 766. See also Millie Allen Beik, *Labor Relations* (Westport, CT: Greenwood, 2005), 249–250; Shostak and Skocik, *The Air Controllers' Controversy*, ch. 6.

40. J. J. Corson, A. W. Bernhard, A. D. Catterson, R. W. Fleming, A. D. Lewis, J. M. Mitchell, and S. H. Ruttenberg, *The Career of the Air Traffic Controller—A Course of Action*, Report of the Air Traffic Control Career Committee (Washington, DC: U.S. Department of Transportation, Office of the Secretary of Transportation, January 1970).

41. See Sylvia Tesh, "The Politics of Stress: The Case of Air Traffic Control," *International Journal of Health Services* 14, no. 4 (1984): 569–587.

42. Meltzer and Sunstein, "Public Employee Strikes, Executive Discretion, and the Air Traffic Controllers," 749–751.

43. Shostak and Skocik, *The Air Controllers' Controversy*, 84–85; McCartin, *Collision Course*, 240.

44. Steven F. Hayward, *The Age of Reagan: The Conservative Counterrevolution 1980–1989* (New York: Three Rivers, 2009), 171.

45. McCartin, *Collision Course*, 246.

46. Evelyn S. Taylor, *P.A.T.C.O. and Reagan: An American Tragedy* (Bloomington, IN: AuthorHouse, 2011), 1.

47. McCartin, *Collision Course*, 248–249.

48. Herbert R. Northrup, "The Rise and Demise of PATCO," 169–171.

49. Meltzer and Sunstein, "Public Employee Strikes, Executive Discretion, and the Air Traffic Controllers," 732.

CHAPTER 2. THE CAST OF CHARACTERS

1. Douglas B. Feaver, "Drew Lewis Is Leaving Cabinet Job," *Washington Post*, December 29, 1982.

2. Emily Langer, "Drew Lewis, Transportation Secretary during Air Traffic Controllers Strike, Dies at 84," *Washington Post*, February 12, 2016.

3. Langer, "Drew Lewis."

4. Joseph A. McCartin, *Collision Course: Ronald Reagan, the Air Traffic Controllers, and the Strike that Changed America* (New York: Oxford University Press, 2011), 256.

5. McCartin, *Collision Course*, 256–257.

6. McCartin, *Collision Course*, 256.

7. US Department of Justice, "Attorney General: William French Smith," https://www.justice.gov/ag/bio/smith-william-french; UVA Miller Center, "William French Smith, 1981–1985," https://millercenter.org/president/reagan/essays

/smith-1981-attorney-general; Richard D. Lyons, "William French Smith Dies at 73; Reagan's First Attorney General," *New York Times*, October 30, 1990, https://www.nytimes.com/1990/10/30/obituaries/william-french-smith-dies-at-73-reagan-s-first-attorney-general.html.

8. Sidney Blumenthal, "David Stockman: The President's Cutting Edge," *New York Times*, March 15, 1981, https://www.nytimes.com/1981/03/15/magazine/david-stockman-the-president-s-cutting-edge.html.

9. Caryle Murphy, "The Boss: Donald Devine: The Man Federal Workers Love to Hate," *Washington Post*, April 15, 1984.

10. US Office of Personnel Management, "Donald Devine," https://www.opm.gov/about-us/our-mission-role-history/agency-leadership/donald-devine/.

11. See Hoover Institution, Remembering Martin Anderson, January 5, 2015, https://www.hoover.org/news/remembering-martin-anderson; Martin Anderson, *Revolution* (New York: Harcourt Brace Jovanovich, 1988).

12. Howell Raines, "Reagan Sticks to Agenda That Won Him the Election," *New York Times*, March 8, 1981.

13. Anderson, *Revolution*, 116.

14. Gerald M. Boyd, "Working Profile: Craig L. Fuller; The Vice President's New Right-Hand Man," *New York Times*, May 21, 1985, https://www.nytimes.com/1985/05/21/us/working-profile-graig-l-fuller-the-vice-president-s-new-right-hand-man.html.

15. Lou Chibbaro, Jr., "Reagan Adviser, Log Cabin Supporter Bob Bonitati Dies at 79," *The Blade*, November 15, 2017, https://www.washingtonblade.com/2017/11/15/reagan-adviser-bob-bonitati-dies/.

16. Adam Clymer, "Richard Wirthlin, Pollster Who Advised Reagan, Dies at 80," *New York Times*, March 17, 2011, https://www.nytimes.com/2011/03/18/us/politics/18wirthlin.html; Richard Wirthlin, *The Greatest Communicator: What Ronald Reagan Taught Me about Politics, Leadership, and Life* (New York: John Wiley & Sons, 2004).

17. Richard Nixon Presidential Library and Museum, "David Gergen Biographical Note," https://www.nixonlibrary.gov/finding-aids/david-r-gergen-white-house-special-files-staff-member-and-office-files.

18. Dom Bonafede, "The Men Around Reagan," in *Ronald Reagan's America*, vol. 2, eds. Eric J. Schmertz, Natalie Datlof, and Alexej Ugrinsky (Westport, CT: Greenwood, 1997), 502.

19. Bonafede, "The Men Around Reagan," 504.

20. Bonafede, "The Men Around Reagan," 502.

21. Ronald Reagan, *An American Life: The Autobiography* (New York: Simon & Shuster, 1990), 161–162.

22. Anderson, *Revolution*, 189.

23. Richard Nathan, *The Administrative Presidency* (New York: Wiley, 1983). For a more detailed examination of the policymaking processes of the Reagan White House, see Anderson, *Revolution*, 191–272.

24. Peter M. Benda and Charles H. Levine, "Reagan and the Bureaucracy: The

Bequest, the Promise, and the Legacy," in *The Reagan Legacy*, ed. Charles O. Jones (Chatham, NJ: Chatham House, 1988), 102. See also Donald J. Devine, *Reagan's Terrible Swift Sword* (Ottawa, IL: Jameson, 1991).

25. McCartin, *Collision Course*.

26. Willis J. Nordlund, *Silent Skies: The Air Traffic Controllers' Strike* (Westport, CT: Praeger, 1999), 72.

27. McCartin, *Collision Course*, 173–174, 220–221, 228, 240.

28. Herbert R. Northrup, "Labor Policies of the Reagan Administration," in *Ronald Reagan's America*, vol. 1, eds. Eric J. Schmertz, Natalie Datlof, and Alexej Ugrinsky (Westport, CT: Greenwood, 1997), 320–321.

29. McCartin, *Collision Course*, 236–237.

30. House of Representatives, "The Honorable William Lacy Clay Sr.," https://history.house.gov/Oral-History/Rainey/Representative-Clay-Sr/.

31. See Robert McNamara, "Tip O'Neill, Powerful Democratic Speaker of the House," ThoughtCo., February 17, 2019, https://www.thoughtco.com/tip-o-neill-4582706.

32. Joseph P. Fried, "Thomas Platt, 91, Dies: Fined Air Traffic Controllers $100,000 an Hour," *New York Times*, March 6, 2017, https://www.nytimes.com/2017/03/06/nyregion/thomas-platt-judge-who-fined-striking-air-traffic-controllers-dies.html; Robert D. Hershey Jr., "Harold H. Greene, Judge Who Oversaw the Breakup of the AT&T Colossus, Dies at 76," *New York Times*, January 30, 2000, https://www.nytimes.com/2000/01/30/nyregion/harold-h-greene-judge-who-oversaw-the-breakup-of-the-at-t-colossus-dies-at-76.html.

33. AFL-CIO, "Lane Kirkland," https://aflcio.org/about/history/labor-history-people/lane-kirkland.

34. AFL-CIO, "Lane Kirkland," https://aflcio.org/about/history/labor-history-people/lane-kirkland; William Serrin, "Lane Kirkland, Who Led Labor in Difficult Times, Is Dead at 77," *New York Times*, August 15, 1999, https://www.nytimes.com/1999/08/15/us/lane-kirkland-who-led-labor-in-difficult-times-is-dead-at-77.html. For a detailed treatment, see Arch Puddington, *Lane Kirkland: Champion of American Labor* (New York: Wiley, 2005).

35. Air Line Pilots Association, International, "Two ALPA Leaders Fly West," April 2022, https://www.alpa.org/news-and-events/air-line-pilot-magazine/alpa-leaders-fly-west; Air Line Pilots Association, International, "Amplifying Our Voice in Washington, D.C.," June 2019, https://www.alpa.org/news-and-events/air-line-pilot-magazine/alpa-pac-amplifying-our-voice.

CHAPTER 3. PRESIDENTIAL DECISION

1. Herbert R. Northrup, "The Rise and Demise of PATCO," *Industrial and Labor Relations Review* 37, no. 2 (January 1984): 174–178.

2. Katherine Newman, *Falling from Grace* (New York: Vintage Books, 1988), 145; Willis J. Nordlund, *Silent Skies: The Air Traffic Controllers Strike* (Westport, CT: Praeger, 1998), 92.

3. "Letter from Richard J. Leighton to Michael Balzano," SRF PATCO document number 3. The letter, styled a "letter of understanding," was read over the phone by Leighton, PATCO Counsel, to Balzano, a Reagan campaign worker. Balzano had the dictation typed and put in the PATCO file, unsigned by Leighton.

4. Bernard D. Meltzer and Cass R. Sunstein, "Public Employee Strikes, Executive Discretion, and the Air Traffic Controllers," *University of Chicago Law Review* 50, no. 2 (Spring 1983): 751.

5. Joseph A. McCartin, *Collision Course: Ronald Reagan, the Air Traffic Controllers, and the Strike That Changed America* (New York: Oxford, 2011), 252, 254.

6. "Letter from Edwin L. Harper to William E. Dannemeyer," April 29, 1981, document number 7, SRF PATCO [4/29/81 Harper Letter, Bonitati, PATCO 4/4]; Evelyn S. Taylor, *P.A.T.C.O. and Reagan: An American Tragedy* (Bloomington, IN: Author House, 2011), 7; Millie Allen Beik, *Labor Relations* (Westport, CT: Greenwood Press, 2005), 252.

7. Richard W. Hurd and Jill K. Kreisky, "'The Rise and Demise of PATCO' Reconstructed," *Industrial and Labor Relations Review* 40, no. 1 (October 1986): 120.

8. McCartin, *Collision Course*, 257-259.

9. Meltzer and Sunstein, "Public Employee Strikes, Executive Discretion, and the Air Traffic Controllers," 754.

10. Nordlund, *Silent Skies*, 90.

11. "1981 Professional Air Traffic Controllers Organization Negotiations, February 7, 1981," SRF PATCO document number 5, [2/7/81, "1981 PATCO Negotiations," Bonitati, PATCO, 4/4].

12. "Letter from Edward P. Faberman to Kenneth Crib," SRF PATCO document number 14.

13. McCartin, *Collision Course*, 260-261.

14. "Statement by Secretary Drew Lewis, June 17, 1981," SRF PATCO document number 26, [6/17/81 Lewis Statement, Bonitati PATCO ¾].

15. McCartin, *Collision Course*, 262.

16. Erik Loomis, *A History of America in Ten Strikes* (New York: New Press, 2020), 182-183.

17. "PATCO 6/20/81," David Gergen Files PATCO.

18. The origin of the discovery is contested. Some hold that it is uncertain and speculate that the letter may have been provided to congressional Democrats by someone inside the administration who hoped to forestall further concessions to PATCO, while the *New York Times* reported that the union itself had provided the Leighton letter to a congressional subcommittee. McCartin, *Collision Course*, 272-273; Richard Witkin, "Air Control Union Eases Strike Threat," *New York Times*, June 20, 1981.

19. "Memorandum from Dick Sullivan to Chairman Levitas," June 24, 1981, SRF PATCO document number 29, [6/24/81 Sullivan memo, Fielding, PATCO ½]. See also Nordlund, *Silent Skies*, 197; Evelyn S. Taylor, *P.A.T.C.O. and Reagan: An American Tragedy* (Bloomington, IN: AuthorHouse, 2011), 51n7.

20. McCartin, *Collision Course*, 265-269; Arthur B. Shostak and David Skocik,

The Air Controllers' Controversy: Lessons from the PATCO Strike (New York: Authors Choice, 2006), 86–87.

21. Nordlund, *Silent Skies*, 92.

22. Joseph S. Miller, *"STRIKE! STRIKE! STRIKE!" The Wicked Wine of Democracy: A Memoir of a Political Junkie, 1948–1995* (Seattle: University of Washington Press, 2008), 215–224.

23. Michael R. Adamson, "Reagan and the Economy: Business and Labor, Regulation and Deregulation," in *A Companion to Ronald Reagan*, ed. Andrew L. Johns (New York: Wiley Blackwell, 2015), 155–157.

24. Shostak and Skocik, *The Air Controllers' Controversy*, 87–88.

25. Sources differ on whether the secret ballot was observed in this strike vote. Nordlund and Northrup say it was not. McCartin did not find that to be the case, though he did conclude that the favorable vote probably fell below 80 percent. No written record of the vote tally remains. Nordlund, *Silent Skies*, 95; Northrup, "The Rise and Demise of PATCO," 177; McCartin, *Collision Course*, 286–287.

26. Shostak and Skocik, *The Air Controllers' Controversy*, 92, 222, 224.

27. Hurd and Kreisky, "'The Rise and Demise of PATCO' Reconstructed," 119.

28. For a variety of views on this question, see Nordlund, *Silent Skies*, 93–96; Northrup, "The Rise and Demise of PATCO," 176–177; Hurd and Kreisky, "'The Rise and Demise of PATCO' Reconstructed."

29. "Statement of the Honorable Drew Lewis," Testimony before House Committee on Post Office and Civil Service, Subcommittee on Employment Compensation and Benefits, April 30, 1981, SRF PATCO document number 9, [4/30/81 Lewis Statement, Bonitati, PATCO 4/4]; Meltzer and Sunstein, "Public Employee Strikes, Executive Discretion, and the Air Traffic Controllers," 755–756; "Statement by Secretary Drew Lewis," June 17, 1981, SRF PATCO document number 26; Ronald Reagan, *The Reagan Diaries*, ed. Douglas Brinkley (New York: HarperCollins, 2007), 26; Statement 7/31/81, David Gergen files, PATCO.

30. Michael Round, *Grounded: Reagan and the PATCO Crash* (New York: Garland, 1999), 51.

31. "Letter from Norman Y. Mineta to Robert E. Poli, June 1, 1981," SRF PATCO document number 18.

32. Transcript, June 1981, Fred Fielding, PATCO file ½.

33. David Morgan, "Terminal Flight: The Air Traffic Controllers' Strike of 1981," *Journal of American Studies* 18, no. 2 (August 1984): 168.

34. Meltzer and Sunstein, "Public Employee Strikes, Executive Discretion, and the Air Traffic Controllers," 757, 757n130.

35. Round, *Grounded*, 35.

36. McCastin, *Collision Course*, 278.

37. William E. Pemberton, *Exit with Honor: The Life and Presidency of Ronald Reagan* (Armonk, NY: M. E. Sharpe, 1997), 107.

38. Shostak and Skocik, *The Air Controllers' Controversy*, 105–106.

39. For cancelled flights and 80 percent figure, see Andrew Glass, "Reagan Fires 11,000 Striking Air Traffic Controllers, Aug. 5, 1981," *Politico*, August 5, 2017,

https://www.politico.com/story/2017/08/05/reagan-fires-11-000-striking-air-tr affic-controllers-aug-5-1981-241252. Loomis, *A History of America in Ten Strikes*, 191; Beik, *Labor Relations*, 254; Northrup, "The Rise and Demise of PATCO," 177; McCartin, *Collision Course*, 301; and others say that around 50 percent of air traffic was maintained on day one of the strike. Nordlund, *Silent Skies*, 197; and Shostak and Skocik, *The Air Controllers' Controversy*, 105 both indicate that 65 percent of air traffic was maintained.

40. "EOP/OMB from Annelise Anderson to Glenn Schleede," June 5, 1981, Fuller PATCO 2/2; Pemberton, *Exit with Honor: The Life and Presidency of Ronald Reagan* (Armonk, NY: M. E. Sharpe, 1998), 107.

41. Dinesh D'Souza, *Ronald Reagan: How an Ordinary Man Became an Extraordinary Leader* (New York: Free Press, 1997), 231.

42. Many of the following considerations can be found in an internal administration analysis of its own June pay and benefits proposal. "Summary of Pay and Benefits: Considerations," Fuller PATCO 2/2. These considerations applied with even greater force to the much higher PATCO demands subsequently.

43. Peggy Noonan, *When Character Was King: A Story of Ronald Reagan* (New York: Penguin, 2002), 223–224.

44. Edwin Meese, *With Reagan* (Washington, DC: Regnery, 1992), 18.

45. Reagan, *The Reagan Diaries*, 26, 34, 35.

46. Meltzer and Sunstein, "Public Employee Strikes, Executive Discretion, and the Air Traffic Controllers," 772–773, and more generally 772–777.

47. Nordlund, *Silent Skies*, 6.

48. Shostak and Skocik, *The Air Controllers' Controversy*, 130.

49. Nordlund, *Silent Skies*, 105–106.

50. Melinda Beck with William J. Cook, "The Crisis Manager," *Newsweek*, August 17, 1981.

51. "Poli Says Reagan Was Misled into Hard-Line Stand," *The Associated Press*, August 16, 1981, https://advance-lexis-com.ccl.idm.oclc.org/api/document?collect ion=news&id=urn:contentItem:3SJ4-M450-0011-41T3-00000-00&context=1516831.

52. Laurence I. Barrett, *Gambling with History: Ronald Reagan in the White House* (Garden City, NY: Doubleday, 1983), 63.

53. Donald J. Devine, *Reagan's Terrible Swift Sword: Reforming and Controlling the Federal Bureaucracy* (Ottawa, IL: Jameson Books, 1991), 84.

54. Peter J. Wallison, *Ronald Reagan: The Power of Conviction and the Success of His Presidency* (Boulder, CO: Westview, 2003), 53.

55. "Notes from 8/3/81 meeting," (mislabeled 7/3/81), David Gergen, 1/2.

56. Bryan Craig, "Reagan vs. Air Traffic Controllers," UVA Miller Center, https://millercenter.org/reagan-vs-air-traffic-controllers.

57. Craig, "Reagan vs. Air Traffic Controllers." It should be noted that Peggy Noonan asserts that Reagan had drafted his statement by hand the night before, but this would seem to be contradicted by Deaver's firsthand account. Noonan, *When Character Was King*, 223.

58. Wallison, *Ronald Reagan*, 53.

59. Ronald Reagan, Remarks and a Question-and-Answer Session with Reporters on the Air Traffic Controllers Strike, August 3, 1981, online by Gerhard Peters and John T. Woolley, The American Presidency Project, https://www.presidency.ucsb.edu/node/246781.

60. Round, *Grounded*, 55-75.

61. Nordlund, *Silent Skies*, 133-135.

62. Round, *Grounded*, 125.

63. Meltzer and Sunstein, "Public Employee Strikes, Executive Discretion, and the Air Traffic Controllers," 781-787.

64. McCartin, *Collision Course*, 301; Millie Allen Beik, *Labor Relations* (Westport, CT: Greenwood, 2005), 254. McCartin sums the total of controllers who were working after the deadline at 4,669, including both controllers who never went on strike and those who returned to work. Beik says 1,300 of those had returned. It is, however, surprisingly difficult to find consensus figures. Though by far the most common figure mentioned by researchers for the number of strikers fired is 11,345, numbers ranging from 11,301 to 11,359 also occasionally appear. The number of PATCO members who initially walked off the job but returned prior to the expiration of the forty-eight-hour deadline is variously reported to have been as low as 845 and as high as 1,600.

65. McCartin, *Collision Course*, 301-302.

66. Beck and Cook, "The Crisis Manager." It also reported that after Reagan left the capital for his California ranch, Lewis "handled the air controllers' strike for five days on his own before Reagan tuned in by telephone." "Home, Home on the Range," *Newsweek*, August 24, 1981, https://advance-lexis-com.ccl.idm.oclc.org/api/document?collection=news&id=urn:contentItem:3SJ4-FK60-0008-X30Y-00000-00&context=1516831.

67. Barrett, *Gambling with History*, 38.

68. Ronald Reagan, *An American Life* (New York: Simon & Schuster, 1991), 282-283.

69. Ronald Reagan, Remarks at a Meeting with Congressional Leaders Following Passage of Federal Budget Reconciliation and Tax Reduction Legislation, August 5, 1981, online by Gerhard Peters and John T. Woolley, The American Presidency Project, https://www.presidency.ucsb.edu/node/246847.

70. "Memorandum to Martin Anderson from William Niskanen," August 6, 1981, Anderson PATCO 1; "Memorandum for Martin Anderson from Kevin Hopkins," August 4, 1981, Anderson PATCO 1; "Letter from Norman G. Kurland to Martin Anderson," August 10, 1981, Anderson PATCO 3; "Letter from R.S. Hollingshead to Martin Anderson," August 6, 1981, Anderson PATCO 3.

71. "Memoranda from Fred F. Fielding, PATCO—Proposed Resolution of Strike," August 14, 1981, SRF PATCO document number 38. Noonan also discusses how Kirkland gave the administration behind-the-scenes support. *When Character Was King*, 224-225.

72. McCartin, *Collision Course*, 314.

73. McCartin, *Collision Course*, 314.

74. Noonan, *When Character Was King*, 225.

75. Ronald Reagan, Remarks on Signing the Economic Recovery Tax Act of 1981 and the Omnibus Budget Reconciliation Act of 1981, and a Question-and-Answer Session with Reporters, August 13, 1981, online by Gerhard Peters and John T. Woolley, The American Presidency Project, https://www.presidency.ucsb.edu/node/246919.

76. *Federal Labor-Management Relations and Impasses Procedures*, Subcommittee on Investigations, Committee on Post Office and Civil Service, House of Representatives, US (Washington, DC: Government Printing Office, 1983), 24.

77. McCartin, *Collision Course*, 315, 318.

78. "Memorandum from Edward C. Schmults to Fred F. Fielding," September 3, 1981, SRF PATCO document number 41.

79. Meltzer and Sunstein, "Public Employee Strikes, Executive Discretion, and the Air Traffic Controllers," 789.

80. Quoted in Shostak and Slocik, *The Air Controllers' Controversy*, 132.

81. Nordlund, *Silent Skies*, 138–139.

82. Shostak and Skocik, *The Air Controllers' Controversy*, 220–221.

83. Joseph Slater, "Strikes in Essential Services in the USA," in *Regulating Strikes in Essential Services: A Comparative 'Law In Action' Perspective*, eds. Moti Mironi and Monika Schlacter (Netherlands: Wolters-Kluwer, 2019), 492; Shostak and Skocik, *The Air Controllers' Controversy*, 116; McCartin, *Collision Course*, 335.

84. Meltzer and Sunstein, "Public Employee Strikes, Executive Discretion, and the Air Traffic Controllers," 787–788.

85. Nordlund, *Silent Skies*, 150–151.

86. "Memorandum about Federal Employment of Discharged Air Traffic Controllers, December 9, 1981," https://www.reaganlibrary.gov/archives/speech/statement-federal-employment-discharged-air-traffic-controllers; McCartin, *Collision Course*, 320–324.

87. Shostak and Skocik, *The Air Controllers' Controversy*, 115.

88. Ronald Reagan, Question-and-Answer Session with Students at St. Peter's Catholic Elementary School in Geneva, Illinois, April 15, 1982, online by Gerhard Peters and John T. Woolley, The American Presidency Project, https://www.presidency.ucsb.edu/node/245049.

89. Ronald Reagan, Message to the House of Representatives Returning the Continuing Appropriations Bill without Approval, October 9, 1986, online by Gerhard Peters and John T. Woolley, The American Presidency Project, https://www.presidency.ucsb.edu/node/253989.

90. Robert E. Poli, "Why the Air Controllers' Strike Failed," *New York Times*, January 17, 1982.

91. Miller, "*STRIKE! STRIKE! STRIKE!*", 215–224.

92. Shostak and Skocik, *The Air Controllers' Controversy*, 216–217.

93. Reagan, *An American Life*, 283.

94. Shostak and Skocik, *The Air Controllers' Controversy*, 114; McCartin, *Collision Course*, 279.

CHAPTER 4. POLITICAL REACTION

1. One poll taken in July 1981 showed that, by a 2-1 margin, Americans believed Reagan's tax and spending cuts would help the economy. Cambridge Reports/Research International, Cambridge Reports/Research International Poll: July 1981, Question 7, USCAMREP.81JUL.R014, Cambridge Reports/Research International (Ithaca, NY: Roper Center for Public Opinion Research, 1981). Another July survey showed 58 percent in favor of Reagan's tax cut, 19 percent opposed. Associated Press/NBC News, NBC News/Associated Press Poll: Federal Spending/Crime, Question 12, USNBCAP.68.R12, Associated Press/NBC News (Ithaca, NY: Roper Center for Public Opinion Research, 1981).

2. Michael Round, *Grounded: Reagan and the PATCO Crash* (New York: Garland, 1999), 50.

3. On August 4, White House phone calls were reported as 1,390 for the president's position, seventy-seven against. On August 6, White House phone calls favored the president 595 to 239; a large proportion of "anti" calls were judged to be the result of an organized effort by PATCO wives. Telegrams ran 2,188 for the president's position, 193 against; mailgrams 966 for, 113 against. "PATCO Developments," Gergen PATCO ½.

4. Rebecca Pels, "The Pressures of PATCO: Strikes and Stress in the 1980s," *Essays in History* 37, no. 8 (January 1995): 1–18.

5. *Newsweek*, *Newsweek* Poll: August 1981, Question 3, USGALNEW.081781.R3, Gallup Organization (Ithaca, NY: Roper Center for Public Opinion Research, 1981).

6. *Newsweek*, *Newsweek* Poll: August 1981, Question 4, USGALNEW.081781.R4, Gallup Organization (Ithaca, NY: Roper Center for Public Opinion Research, 1981).

7. *Newsweek*, *Newsweek* Poll: August 1981, Question 2, USGALNEW.081781.R2, Gallup Organization (Ithaca, NY: Roper Center for Public Opinion Research, 1981).

8. Associated Press/NBC News, NBC News/Associated Press Poll: Reagan/Politics, Question 13, USNBCAP.69.R15, Associated Press/NBC News (Ithaca, NY: Roper Center for Public Opinion Research, 1981).

9. Associated Press/NBC News, NBC News/Associated Press Poll: Reagan/Politics, Question 16, USNBCAP.69.R16C, Associated Press/NBC News (Ithaca, NY: Roper Center for Public Opinion Research, 1981).

10. Louis Harris & Associates, Louis Harris & Associates Poll: August 1981, Question 9, USHARRIS.082081.R09, Louis Harris & Associates (Ithaca, NY: Roper Center for Public Opinion Research, 1981).

11. Louis Harris & Associates, Louis Harris & Associates Poll: August 1981, Question 10, USHARRIS.082081.R10, Louis Harris & Associates (Ithaca, NY: Roper Center for Public Opinion Research, 1981).

12. Louis Harris & Associates, Louis Harris & Associates Poll: August 1981, Question 1, USHARRIS.082081.R01, Louis Harris & Associates (Ithaca, NY: Roper Center for Public Opinion Research, 1981).

13. Gallup Organization, Gallup Poll #1181G, Question 8, USGALLUP.1181. Q04D, Gallup Organization (Ithaca, NY: Roper Center for Public Opinion Research, 1981).

14. Gallup Organization, Gallup Poll #1181G, Question 18, USGALLUP.1181. Q06F, Gallup Organization (Ithaca, NY: Roper Center for Public Opinion Research, 1981).

15. The Roper Organization, Roper Reports 1981-08: Economy/Business, Question 14, USROPER.81-8.R03X, The Roper Organization (Ithaca, NY: Roper Center for Public Opinion Research, 1981).

16. The Roper Organization, Roper Reports 1981-08: Economy/Business, Question 124, USROPER.81-8.R45XJ, The Roper Organization (Ithaca, NY: Roper Center for Public Opinion Research, 1981).

17. The Roper Organization, Roper Reports 1981-08: Economy/Business, Question 12, USROPER.81-8.R02KX, The Roper Organization (Ithaca, NY: Roper Center for Public Opinion Research, 1981).

18. *Time Magazine,* Yankelovich/*Time Magazine* Poll: Time Soundings—Political Leaders/Foreign Policy, Question 65, USYANK.818608.Q08B, Yankelovich, Skelly & White (Ithaca, NY: Roper Center for Public Opinion Research, 1981).

19. William E. Pemberton, *Exit with Honor: The Life and Presidency of Ronald Reagan* (Armonk, NY: M. E. Sharpe, 1999), 107.

20. Associated Press/NBC News, Associated Press/NBC News Poll: December 1981, Question 18, USNBCAP.73.R18, Associated Press/NBC News (Ithaca, NY: Roper Center for Public Opinion Research, 1981).

21. Robert E. Poli, "Why the Air Controllers' Strike Failed," *New York Times*, January 17, 1982.

22. Bernard D. Meltzer and Cass R. Sunstein, "Public Employee Strikes, Executive Discretion, and the Air Traffic Controllers," *University of Chicago Law Review* 50, no. 2 (Spring 1983): 760-761.

23. Katherine S. Newman, "PATCO Lives! Stigma, Heroism, and Symbolic Transformations," *Cultural Anthropology* 2, no. 3 (1987): 319-346.

24. Arthur B. Shostak and David Skocik, *The Air Controllers' Controversy: Lessons from the PATCO Strike* (New York: Authors Choice, 2006), 104.

25. Shostak and Skocik, *The Air Controllers' Controversy*, 222.

26. Gallup Organization, "Presidential Job Approval Center," https://news.gallup.com/interactives/185273/presidential-job-approval-center.aspx.

27. ABC News, ABC News Poll: September 1981, ABC News (Ithaca, NY: Roper Center for Public Opinion Research, 1981); ABC News/*Washington Post*, ABC News/*Washington Post* Poll: July 1981, ABC News/*Washington Post* (Ithaca, NY: Roper Center for Public Opinion Research, 1981).

28. *Newsweek, Newsweek* Poll: August 1981, Question 5, USGALNEW.081781. R5, Gallup Organization (Ithaca, NY: Roper Center for Public Opinion Research, 1981).

29. Evelyn S. Taylor, *P.A.T.C.O. and Reagan: An American Tragedy* (Bloomington, IN: AuthorHouse, 2011), 27.

30. Associated Press/NBC News, Associated Press/NBC News Poll: December 1981, Question 20, USNBCAP.73.R20, Associated Press/NBC News (Ithaca, NY: Roper Center for Public Opinion Research, 1981).

31. David Morgan, "Terminal Flight: The Air Traffic Controllers' Strike of 1981," *Journal of American Studies* 18, no. 2 (August 1984): 181.

32. Taylor, *P.A.T.C.O. and Reagan: An American Tragedy*, 28.

33. Taylor, *P.A.T.C.O. and Reagan: An American Tragedy*, 28.

34. For comments by all the following senators, see *Congressional Record—Senate*, August 3, 1981, 19296–19297, 19299, 19339.

35. For comments by Downey, Oakar, Ritter, Coughlin, and Conyers, See *Congressional Record—House of Representatives*, August 4, 1981, 19493, 19497.

36. John Conyers, "The Air Controllers Strike Should Be Legalized," *New York Times*, August 7, 1981.

37. "Another Threat of Airline Chaos," *Newsweek*, August 10, 1981.

38. "Lewis Vows U.S. Won't Rehire Striking Controllers," Associated Press, August 14, 1981, https://advance-lexis-com.ccl.idm.oclc.org/api/document?collection=news&id=urn:contentItem:3SJ4-M4D0-0011-42BP-00000-00&context=1516831.

39. Morgan, "Terminal Flight," 175–176.

40. Tom Mackaman, "Forty Years since the PATCO Strike: Part Four," World Wide Socialist Web, August 8, 2021, https://www.wsws.org/en/articles/2021/08/09/patc-a09.html.

41. Chris Matthews, *Tip and the Gipper: When Politics Worked* (New York: Simon & Schuster, 2013), 167; Joseph A. McCartin, *Collision Course: Ronald Reagan, the Air Traffic Controllers, and the Strike That Changed America* (New York: Oxford University Press, 2011), 284, 307.

42. Matthews, *Tip and the Gipper*, 167.

43. See Tip O'Neill with William Novak, *Man of the House: The Life and Political Memoirs of Tip O'Neill* (New York: Random House, 1987); John Aloysius Farrell, *Tip O'Neill and the Democratic Century* (Boston: Little, Brown, 2001).

44. Taylor, *P.A.T.C.O. and Reagan: An American Tragedy*, 28–29.

45. Morgan, "Terminal Flight," 174.

46. "Letter from Paul Ignatius to Robert E. Poli, May 28, 1981," SRF PATCO document number 17 [5/29/81 Ignatius Letter, Bonitati, PATCO 4/4].

47. Willis J. Nordlund, *Silent Skies: The Air Traffic Controllers' Strike* (New York: Praeger, 1998), 109.

48. Meltzer and Sunstein, "Public Employee Strikes, Executive Discretion, and the Air Traffic Controllers," 789–794.

49. Nordlund, *Silent Skies*, 140–142, 146.

50. Mackaman, "Forty Years since the PATCO Strike."

51. "Bring the Controllers Down to Earth," *New York Times*, June 19, 1981.

52. "Holding Up America," *New York Times*, August 4, 1981.

53. Cited in Round, *Grounded*, 36.

54. "Struck Out," *Washington Post*, August 4, 1981, https://www.washington

post.com/archive/politics/1981/08/04/struck-out/4f4b5110-7b2c-47af-8aff-3b8c9a549fc1/.

55. *New York Daily News*, August 6, 1981, cited in Shostak and Skocik, *The Air Controllers' Controversy*, 109–110.

56. *Atlanta Journal-Constitution*, August 4, 1981; *Portland Oregon Journal*, August 7, 1981. Reprinted in *Editorials on File* 12, no. 15 (August 1–15, 1981): 886.

57. "Strike Looks Like Disaster for PATCO: Union Has Little Support from Outside," *Chicago Tribune*, August 5, 1981.

58. "No Room for Compromise," *Wall Street Journal*, August 6, 1981.

59. *Fort Worth Star-Telegram*, August 12, 1981.

60. See *Editorials on File*, August 1–15, 1981, 886–895.

61. "Sea-change for Labor," *Boston Globe*, August 12, 1981.

62. "The Sky after PATCO," *Boston Globe*, October 16, 1981.

63. For more examples of the former, see the *Lincoln Star*, the *Des Moines Register*, and the *Cleveland Plain Dealer*. Reprinted in *Editorials on File*, August 1–15, 1981, 886, 888–889, and 890.

64. William Randolph Hearst Jr., "Editor's Report," *San Francisco Chronicle and Examiner*, August 9, 1981.

65. "Time to Think about Clemency," *San Francisco Chronicle and Examiner*, August 30, 1981.

66. "Compassion and the Towers," *Los Angeles Times*, September 16, 1981.

67. Morgan, "Terminal Flight," 180.

68. McCartin, *Collision Course*, 306.

69. "Traffic Snarl," *The New Republic*, August 22 & 29, 1981.

70. "The Great Airport Robbery," *National Review*, August 21, 1981.

71. James Kilpatrick, "They Struck a Blow for Tyranny," *National Review*, October 2, 1981. The magazine also published at least two additional pro-Reagan and anti-PATCO pieces in the aftermath of the strike. See "Labor Lessons," *National Review*, September 4, 1981; "Think Again, Lane Kirkland," *National Review*, October 30, 1981.

72. Steven F. Hayward, *The Age of Reagan: The Conservative Counterrevolution 1980–1989* (New York: Three Rivers, 2009), 173–174.

73. William Raspberry, "PATCO Deserves a Gift," *Washington Post*, December 7, 1981.

74. Morgan, "Terminal Flight," 180, 183.

75. Poli, "Why the Air Controllers' Strike Failed."

76. Nordlund, *Silent Skies*, 116.

77. Shostak and Skocik, *The Air Controllers' Controversy*, 106.

78. Morgan, "Terminal Flight," 171, 179.

79. Nordlund, *Silent Skies*, 106–112.

80. Erik Loomis, *A History of America in Ten Strikes* (New York: New Press, 2020), 191.

81. Shostak and Skocik, *The Air Controllers' Controversy*, 107.

82. Shostak and Skocik, *The Air Controllers' Controversy*, 107–108.

83. Eric Pianin et al., "250,000 March to Protest Reagan's Policies," *Washington Post*, September 20, 1981, https://www.washingtonpost.com/archive/politics/1981/09/20/250000-march-to-protest-reagans-policies/680f4df6-905b-443a-859f-10d8fd3c6a04/; Nordlund, *Silent Skies*, 125. For an in-depth examination of Solidarity Day, see Timothy J. Minchin, "Together We Shall Be Heard: Exploring the 1981 'Solidarity Day' Mass March," *Labor* 12, no. 3 (September 1, 2015): 75–96, https://doi.org/10.1215/15476715-2920376.

84. McCartin, *Collision Course*, 318–319; Morgan, "Terminal Flight," 179; Shostak and Skocik, *The Air Controllers' Controversy*, 128; Mackaman, "Forty Years since the PATCO Strike."

85. Poli, "Why the Air Controllers' Strike Failed."

86. Shostak and Skocik, *The Air Controllers' Controversy*, 115.

87. Nordlund, *Silent Skies*, 111.

88. McCartin, *Collision Course*, 308–309.

89. McCartin, *Collision Course*, 310.

90. McCartin, *Collision Course*, 316–317.

91. Shostak and Skocik, *The Air Controllers' Controversy*, 108.

92. "Traffic Snarl."

93. Herbert R. Northrup, "Labor Policies of the Reagan Administration," in *Ronald Reagan's America*, vol. 1, eds. Eric J. Schmertz, Natalie Datlof, and Alexej Ugrinsky (Westport, CT: Greenwood, 1997), 320–321.

94. Herbert R. Northrup, "The Rise and Demise of PATCO," *Industrial and Labor Relations Review* 37, no. 2 (January 1984): 181; McCartin, *Collision Course*, 311–312.

95. United Press International, August 4, 1981, https://advance-lexis-com.ccl.idm.oclc.org/document/?pdmfid=1516831&crid=872bd082-e3b2-4a96-98d1-78a4520a909b&pddocfullpath=%2Fshared%2Fdocument%2Fnews%2Furn%3AcontentItem%3A3SJB-2660-001X-N17V-00000-00&pdcontentcomponentid=8076&pdteaserkey=sr5&pditab=allpods&ecomp=kmnyk&earg=sr5&prid=47d49151-c5d0-4781-8211-28ff77676eb7.

96. McCartin, *Collision Course*, 304–305.

97. Morgan, "Terminal Flight," 170.

98. Nordlund, *Silent Skies*, 114–115; Morgan, "Terminal Flight," 176–177.

99. Patricia Koza, *United Press International*, August 4, 1981, https://advance-lexis-com.ccl.idm.oclc.org/api/document?collection=news&id=urn:contentItem:3SJB-2650-001X-N16K-00000-00&context=1516831.

100. WHORL PA 13, casefile 142021.

101. Stuart Taylor Jr., "U.S. Officials Shun Conflict in Talks to Bar Group," *New York Times*, August 11, 1981, https://advance-lexis-com.ccl.idm.oclc.org/api/document?collection=news&id=urn:contentItem:3S8G-F660-000B-Y26X-00000-00&context=1516831; William French Smith, *Law and Justice in the Reagan Administration: The Memoirs of an Attorney General* (Stanford, CA: Hoover Institution, 1991), 246.

CHAPTER 5. CONSEQUENCES

1. Katherine S. Newman, "PATCO Lives! Stigma, Heroism, and Symbolic Transformations," *Cultural Anthropology* 2, no. 3 (August 1987): 319–346. See also Arthur B. Shostak and David Skocik, *The Air Controllers' Controversy: Lessons from the PATCO Strike* (New York: Authors Choice, 2006), 131–158.

2. Joseph A. McCartin, *Collision Course: Ronald Reagan, The Air Traffic Controllers, and the Strike That Changed America* (New York: Oxford University Press, 2011), 332.

3. Herbert R. Northrup, "Labor Policies of the Reagan Administration," in *Ronald Reagan's America* vol. 1, eds. Eric J. Schmertz, Natalie Datlof, and Alexej Ugrinsky (Westport, CT: Greenwood, 1997), 322; McCartin, *Collision Course*, 335. Several years later, a congressional investigation unearthed evidence that FAA officials in Chicago Center, a hotbed of PATCO militancy, had altered documentation to undermine certain appeals. Willis J. Nordlund, *Silent Skies: The Air Traffic Controllers' Strike* (Westport, CT: Praeger, 1998), chapter 8.

4. McCartin, *Collision Course*, 356–357; Andrew Glass, "Reagan Fires 11,000 Striking Air Traffic Controllers, Aug. 5, 1981," *Politico*, August 5, 2017.

5. McCartin, *Collision Course*, 352–355, 368–369; Shostak and Skocik, *The Air Controllers' Controversy*, 161–174.

6. Nordlund, *Silent Skies*, 155.

7. McCartin, *Collision Course*, 305.

8. Nordlund, *Silent Skies*, 122.

9. Nordlund, *Silent Skies*, 149–150, 124.

10. "FAA Report: Fewer Near-Misses," *San Francisco Chronicle*, August 19, 1981.

11. William J. Lanovette, "Sending Labor a Message," *National Journal*, August 22, 1981, 1516.

12. McCartin, *Collision Course*, 290, 300; concurring with McCartin, see also Erik Loomis, *A History of America in Ten Strikes* (New York: New Press, 2018); Millie Allen Beik, *Labor Relations* (Westport, CT: Greenwood, 2005), 256.

13. Loomis, *A History of America in Ten Strikes*, 184.

14. Nordlund, *Silent Skies*, 190.

15. McCartin, *Collision Course*, 338–339.

16. Northrup, "Labor Policies of the Reagan Administration," 322; "Around the Nation: Postal Workers Approve New Pact by Large Margin," *New York Times*, August 25, 1981.

17. Peter Perl, "Big Postal Unions Vote Against a Strike, Favor Arbitration," *Washington Post*, August 21, 1984, https://www.washingtonpost.com/archive/politics/1984/08/21/big-postal-unions-vote-against-a-strike-favor-arbitration/395db864-8525-4d34-890d-708e14c11151/.

18. Nordlund, *Silent Skies*, 125.

19. McCartin, *Collision Course*, 339–340, 365.

20. Herbert R. Northrup, "The Rise and Demise of PATCO," *Industrial and Labor Relations Review* 37, no. 2 (January 1984): 167.

21. McCartin, *Collision Course*, 340–341.

22. See Jude Schwalbach, "How Teacher Unions Failed Students during the Pandemic," The Witherspoon Institute, April 4, 2022, https://www.thepublicdiscourse.com/2022/04/81397/; Kerry McDonald, "Teachers Unions Continue to Block School Reopenings across America," Foundation for Economic Education, February 5, 2021, https://fee.org/articles/teachers-unions-continue-to-block-school-reopenings-across-america/.

23. Michael Barone, *Our Country: The Shaping of America from Roosevelt to Reagan* (New York: Free Press, 1991), 617. See also Michael A. Genovese, Todd L. Belt, and William W. Lammers, *The Presidency and Domestic Policy: Comparing Leadership Styles, FDR to Obama*, 2nd ed. (Boulder: Paradigm, 2014), 97, where the authors note that "[Reagan's] actions appeared to demonstrate the merits of a hard line on labor-management disputes. That attitude permeated decisions by the National Labor Relations Board during the Reagan years and encouraged management to take a hard line on strikes."

24. "Discussant: William Krupman," and Herbert R. Northrup, "Labor Policies of the Reagan Administration," both in *Ronald Reagan's America*, 332.

25. Michael H. Leroy, "The Changing Character of Strikes Involving Permanent Striker Replacements, 1935–1990," *Journal of Labor Research* 16: 423–437.

26. Michael R. Adamson, "Reagan and the Economy: Business and Labor, Deregulation and Regulation," in *A Companion to Ronald Reagan*, ed. Andrew L. Johns (Oxford: John Wiley & Sons, 2015), 152.

27. For the contours of this debate, see Schmertz, Datlof, and Ugrinsky, *Ronald Reagan's America*, 313–340; Thomas L. Traynor and Rudy H. Fichtenbaum, "The Impact of Post-PATCO Labor Relations on U.S. Wages," *Eastern Economic Journal* 23, no. 1 (Winter 1997): 61–72; Henry S. Farber and Bruce Western, "Ronald Reagan and the Politics of Declining Union Organization," Working Paper #460, Princeton University, Industrial Relations Section, December 2001; Shostak and Skocik, *The Air Controllers' Controversy*; Leroy, "The Changing Character of Strikes Involving Permanent Striker Replacements, 1935–1990"; Richard W. Hurd and Jill K. Kreisky, "'The Rise and Demise of PATCO' Reconstructed," *Industrial and Labor Relations Review* 40, no. 1 (October 1986): 121.

28. Jon Schwartz, "The Murder of the U.S. Middle Class Began 40 Years Ago This Week," *The Intercept*, August 6, 2021, https://theintercept.com/2021/08/06/middle-class-reagan-patco-strike/.

29. See for example Lee E. Ohanian, "Competition and the Decline of the Rust Belt," Federal Reserve Bank of Minneapolis, December 20, 2014, https://www.minneapolisfed.org/article/2014/competition-and-the-decline-of-the-rust-belt; Simeon Alder, David Lagakos, and Lee Ohanian, "Competitive Pressure and the Decline of the Rust Belt: A Macroeconomic Analysis," Working Paper #20538, National Bureau of Economic Research, October 2014, https://www.nber.org/system/files/working_papers/w20538/w20538.pdf. For a contrary view, see Thomas Karier, "Trade Deficits and Labor Unions: Myths and Realities," Economic Policy Institute, n.d., https://www.iatp.org/sites/default/files/Trade_Deficits_and_Labor_Unions_Myths_and_Real.htm.

30. John Crudele, "Decline of Unionism Didn't Start with PATCO Strike," *St. Louis Post-Dispatch*, June 3, 1991.

31. Donald J. Devine, *Reagan's Terrible Swift Sword: Reforming and Controlling the Federal Bureaucracy* (Ottawa, IL: Jameson Books, 1991), 84.

32. Peter J. Wallison, *Ronald Reagan: The Power of Conviction and the Success of His Presidency* (Boulder, CO: Westview, 2003), 54.

33. The Federal Reserve Board, remarks by Chairman Alan Greenspan, *The Reagan Legacy*, at the Ronald Reagan Library, Simi Valley, California, April 9, 2003, https://www.federalreserve.gov/boarddocs/speeches/2003/200304092/default.htm.

34. *Commanding Heights*, "Paul Volcker," PBS, aired September 26, 2000, https://www.pbs.org/wgbh/commandingheights/shared/minitext/int_paulvolcker.html#6.

35. "Discussant: Theodore W. Kheel," and Herbert R. Northrup, "Labor Policies of the Reagan Administration," both in *Ronald Reagan's America*, 328.

36. Northrup, "The Labor Policies of the Reagan Administration," 322n28.

37. Lawrence Mishel, Lynn Rhinehart, and Lane Windham, "Explaining the Erosion of Private-sector Unions," Economic Policy Institute, Table A, November 18, 2020, https://www.epi.org/unequalpower/publications/private-sector-unions-corporate-legal-erosion/.

38. Mishel, Rhinehart, and Windham, "Explaining the Erosion of Private-sector Unions."

39. Kim Moody, "A Pattern of Retreat: The Decline of Pattern Bargaining," February 16, 2010, https://labornotes.org/2010/02/pattern-retreat-decline-pattern-bargaining.

40. Steve Fraser, *The Age of Acquiescence: The Life and Death of American Resistance to Organized Wealth and Power* (New York: Basic Books, 2016). See James N. Larkin, "5 Vital Lessons from American Labor's Rise and Fall," *The Nation*, September 15, 2015, https://www.thenation.com/article/archive/the-fate-of-americas-unions/.

41. The White House, "The State of Our Unions," September 5, 2022, https://www.whitehouse.gov/cea/written-materials/2022/09/05/the-state-of-our-unions/.

42. Adamson, "Reagan and the Economy," 157.

43. "Discussant: Bernard Plum," and Herbert R. Northrup, "Labor Policies of the Reagan Administration," both in *Ronald Reagan's America*, 333.

44. Godfrey Hodgson, *The World Turned Right Side Up: A History of the Conservative Ascendancy in America* (Boston: Houghton Mifflin, 1996), 246.

45. John Lippert, "Decade Later, Strike Haunts Air Controllers and Labor," *Detroit Free Press*, July 28, 1991, cited in Michael Barera, "The 1981 PATCO Strike," UTA Libraries, September 2, 2021, libraries.uta.edu/news-events/blog/1981-patco-strike.

46. See Ed Townsend, "Workers Didn't Wear a Union Label at Polls," *Christian Science Monitor*, November 8, 1984, https://www.csmonitor.com/1984/1108/110836.html.

47. Paul R. Abrahamson, John H. Aldrich, and David W. Rohde, *Change and Continuity in the 1984 Elections*, revised ed. (Washington, DC: CQ, 1987), 136–137.

48. Phil Gailey, "A.F.L.-C.I.O. Chiefs Support Mondale for '84 Nomination," *New York Times*, October 2, 1983, https://www.nytimes.com/1983/10/02/us/afl-cio-chiefs-support-mondale-for-84-nomination.html.

49. Benjamin Ginsberg and Martin Shefter, "The Presidency, Interest Groups, and Social Forces: Creating a Republican Coalition," in *The Presidency and the Political System*, 3rd ed., ed. Michael Nelson (Washington, DC: CQ, 1990), 143–146.

50. Ginsberg and Shefter, "The Presidency, Interest Groups, and Social Forces."

51. Ruy Teixeira, "White Liberals Vs. the Working Class," The Liberal Patriot, February 9, 2023, https://www.liberalpatriot.com/p/white-liberals-vs-the-working-class?utm_source=substack&utm_medium=email.

52. Robert Dallek, *Ronald Reagan: The Politics of Symbolism* (Cambridge: Harvard University Press, 1999), 92.

53. To Hugh Heclo, "Reagan was probably the only twentieth-century president whose political career was so thoroughly devoted to contesting for the public philosophy." Heclo, "Reagan and American Public Philosophy," in *The Reagan Presidency: Pragmatic Conservatism and Its Legacies*, eds. W. Elliott Brownlee and Hugh Davis Graham (Lawrence: University Press of Kansas, 2003), 18.

54. Joseph A. McCartin, "The Downward Path We've Trod: Reflections on an Ominous Anniversary," Working-Class Perspectives, August 2021, https://lwp.georgetown.edu/news/wcp-the-downward-path-weve-trod-reflections-on-an-ominous-anniversary.

55. A notable early warning of this danger was issued by Robert D. Putnam in *Bowling Alone: The Collapse and Renewal of American Community* (New York: Simon & Schuster, 2000).

56. Ronald Reagan, *An American Life* (New York: Simon & Schuster, 1990), 283.

57. Dinesh D'Souza, *Ronald Reagan: How an Ordinary Man Became an Extraordinary Leader* (New York: Free Press, 1997), 231.

58. Bryan Craig, "Reagan vs. Air Traffic Controllers," UVA Miller Center, https://millercenter.org/reagan-vs-air-traffic-controllers.

59. Edwin Meese III, *With Reagan: The Inside Story* (Washington, DC: Regnery Gateway, 1992), 17–18.

60. Wallison, *Ronald Reagan*, 52–54.

61. Wallison, *Ronald Reagan*, 54.

62. Craig, "Reagan vs. Air Traffic Controllers."

63. Craig, "Reagan vs. Air Traffic Controllers."

64. Lou Cannon, *President Reagan: The Role of a Lifetime* (New York: Simon & Schuster, 1991), 437, 497.

65. Haynes Johnson, *Sleepwalking Through History: America in the Reagan Years* (New York: W. W. Norton, 1991), 153.

66. *Washington Post*, August 9, 1981; cited by Ceaser below.

67. Adamson, "Reagan and the Economy," 152.

68. Cited by Adamson, "Reagan and the Economy," 152–153.
69. William E. Pemberton, *Exit with Honor: The Life and Presidency of Ronald Reagan* (Armonk, NY: M. E. Sharpe, 1998), 106.
70. Michael Beschloss, *Presidential Courage: Brave Leaders and How They Changed America 1789–1989* (New York: Simon & Schuster, 2007), 287.
71. James W. Ceaser, "The Reagan Presidency and American Public Opinion," in *The Reagan Legacy: Promise and Performance*, ed. Charles O. Jones (Chatham, NJ: Chatham House, 1988), 184.
72. See, for example, Forrest McDonald, *The American Presidency: An Intellectual History* (Lawrence: University Press of Kansas, 1994), 343.
73. Richard E. Neustadt, *Presidential Power and the Modern Presidents: The Politics of Leadership from Roosevelt to Reagan* (New York: Free Press, 1990), 269.
74. Pemberton, *Exit with Honor*, 210.
75. Richard Nathan, "Institutional Change Under Reagan," in *Perspectives on the Reagan Years*, ed. John L. Palmer (Washington, DC: Urban Institute, 1986), 122–123.
76. Lou Cannon, "A New Confidence in the Presidency," *Newsweek*, January 9, 1989.
77. Teresa Ghilarducci, "When Management Strikes: PATCO and the British Miners," *Industrial Relations Journal* 17, no. 2 (Summer 1986): 115–128.
78. Herbert Northrup and Duncan Campbell, "Comment: Did PATCO Really Lead to the British Miners' Strike?," *Industrial Relations Journal* 17, no. 2 (Summer 1986): 154–158.
79. "The Air Strike," *Washington Post*, August 7, 1981, https://www.washingtonpost.com/archive/politics/1981/08/07/the-air-strike/f9223021-98eb-4023-b99e-ff251abe283c/.
80. William Imboden, *The Peacemaker: Ronald Reagan, the Cold War, and the World on the Brink* (New York: Dutton, 2022), 102.
81. Michael Schaller, *Reckoning with Reagan: America and Its President in the 1980s* (New York: Oxford University Press, 1992), 44.
82. Steven F. Hayward, *The Age of Reagan: The Conservative Counterrevolution: 1980–1989* (New York: Three Rivers, 2009), 173.
83. Laurence I. Barrett, *Gambling with History: Ronald Reagan in the White House* (Barden City, NY: Doubleday, 1983), 204.
84. Chris Matthews, *Tip and the Gipper* (New York: Simon & Schuster, 2013), 167–168.
85. McCartin, *Collision Course*, 324.
86. McCartin, *Collision Course*, 329.
87. George P. Shultz, *Turmoil and Triumph: My Years as Secretary of State* (New York: Charles Scribner's Sons, 1993), 1135.
88. Peggy Noonan, *When Character Was King: A Story of Ronald Reagan* (New York: Penguin, 2002), 226.
89. Edmund Morris, *Dutch: A Memoir of Ronald Reagan* (New York: Random House, 1999), 448.

90. "Discussant: Herbert E. Meyer" in *President Reagan and the World*, eds. Eric J. Schmertz, Natalie Datlof, and Alexej Ugrinsky (Westport, CT: Greenwood, 1997), 126.

CONCLUSION

1. William French Smith, *Law and Justice in the Reagan Administration: The Memoirs of an Attorney General* (Stanford: Hoover Institution, 1991), 246.
2. Michael Barone, *Our Country: Roosevelt to Reagan* (New York: Free Press, 1990), 617. See also Steven F. Hayward, *The Age of Reagan: The Conservative Counterrevolution: 1980–1989* (New York: Three Rivers, 2009), 324.
3. Noonan, *When Character was King: A Story of Ronald Reagan* (New York: Penguin, 2002), 227.
4. Herbert R. Northrup, "The Rise and Demise of PATCO," *Industrial and Labor Relations Review* 37, no. 2 (January 1984): 167; "Discussant: Theodore W. Kheel" and Herbert R. Northrup, "Labor Policies of the Reagan Administration," both in *Ronald Reagan's America*, vol. 1, eds. Eric J. Schmertz, Natalie Datlof, and Alexej Ugrinsky (Westport, CT: Greenwood, 1997), 328; Willis J. Nordlund, *Silent Skies: The Air Traffic Controllers' Strike* (Westport, CT: Praeger, 1997), 190; *Commanding Heights*, "Paul Volcker," PBS, aired September 26, 2000, https://www.pbs.org/wgbh/commandingheights/shared/minitext/int_paulvolcker.html#6; Millie Allen Beik, *Labor Relations* (Westport, CT: Greenwood, 2005), 249.
5. Joseph A. McCartin, *Collision Course: Ronald Reagan, the Air Traffic Controllers, and the Strike That Changed America* (New York: Oxford, 2011), 346.
6. The Federal Reserve Board, remarks by Chairman Alan Greenspan, *The Reagan Legacy*, at the Ronald Reagan Library, Simi Valley, California, April 9, 2003, https://www.federalreserve.gov/boarddocs/speeches/2003/200304092/default.htm.
7. James W. Ceaser, "The Reagan Presidency and American Public Opinion," in *The Reagan Legacy: Promise and Performance*, ed. Charles O. Jones (Chatham, NJ: Chatham House, 1988), 184.
8. Peggy Noonan, *When Character Was King: A Story of Ronald Reagan* (New York: Penguin, 2002), 226.
9. "Discussant: William Krupman," and Herbert R. Northrup, "Labor Policies of the Reagan Administration," both in *Ronald Reagan's America*, 332.
10. "The Air Strike," *Washington Post*, August 7, 1981, https://www.washingtonpost.com/archive/politics/1981/08/07/the-air-strike/f9223021-98eb-4023-b99e-ff251abe283c/.

BIBLIOGRAPHIC ESSAY

The book employs a wide-ranging set of sources, starting with a number of books on the strike. The earliest of these was Arthur B. Shostak and David Skocik, *The Air Controllers' Controversy: Lessons from the PATCO Strike*. Written by a member of the striking PATCO (Skocik) and an academic sociologist who eventually joined the new, poststrike PATCO (Shostak), *The Air Controllers' Controversy* provides an inside glimpse into the union and its strategy; it was initially published in 1986, with a new edition in 2006. Along with an account of the strike, Shostak and Skocik include information on ongoing attempts to organize the controllers as well as revealing interviews with key union leaders and activists. Willis J. Nordlund, *Silent Skies: The Air Traffic Controllers' Strike* (1997), and Michael Round, *Grounded: Reagan and the PATCO Crash* (1999), came next. In time for the thirtieth anniversary of the strike, Evelyn S. Taylor published *P.A.T.C.O. and Reagan: An American Tragedy* in 2011. Taylor's book, while short, includes considerable documentary evidence. That same year, award-winning labor historian Joseph A. McCartin published his comprehensive examination of the strike, *Collision Course: Ronald Reagan, the Air Traffic Controllers, and the Strike that Changed America*. *Collision Course* includes nearly 250 pages of material on the founding and development of PATCO prior to 1981 and is an invaluable resource on the union. All but Taylor's book come from a labor perspective, though McCartin also garnered praise for his evenhandedness from conservative reviewers.

A wide range of other sources were also put to use. Numerous journal articles provided useful information and analysis. Within a few years of the strike, Herbert R. Northrup ("The Rise and Demise of PATCO," 1984) faced off in the pages of *Industrial and Labor Relations Review* with Richard W. Hurd and Jill K. Kreisky ("'The Rise and Demise of PATCO' Reconstructed," 1986), the former more skeptical and the latter more sympathetic to the union. Other key journal articles by David Martin ("Terminal Flight," 1984), Bernard D. Meltzer and Cass R. Sunstein ("Public Employees Strikes, Executive Discretion, and the Air Traffic Controllers," 1983), Rebecca Pels ("The Pressures of PATCO," 1995),

Teresa Ghilarducci ("When Management Strikes," 1986), Katherine S. Newman ("PATCO Lives!", 1987), and others were important sources. A number of economics journal articles used in chapter 5 address the economic consequences of firing PATCO strikers and of union activism in the 1970s. Erik Loomis's book *A History of America in Ten Strikes* (2020) and Millie Allen Biek's volume *Labor Relations* (2005) each have chapters addressing the PATCO strike from a pro-union perspective.

Also very useful were memoirs by administration officials including Presidential Counselor Edwin Meese III, Office of Personnel Management Director Donald J. Devine, Attorney General William French Smith, speechwriter Peggy Noonan, White House Legal Counsel Peter Wallison, Secretary of State George Shultz, and of course, Reagan himself. Reagan's diaries and the script of Reagan's syndicated radio broadcasts provide additional insight into Reagan's thinking. I also relied on published interviews with figures such as Michael Deaver and Martin Anderson in the White House, Paul Volcker at the Federal Reserve, and Senators Howard Baker and Paul Laxalt (many of which were oral histories conducted by the Miller Center at the University of Virginia) or published accounts by participants (such as PATCO president Robert E. Poli, who offered his personal analysis in a January 1982 *New York Times* piece entitled "Why the Air Controllers' Strike Failed").

The published proceedings of an April 1993 conference on the Reagan Presidency at Hofstra University provided additional material, as did short sections within book-length accounts of Reagan's presidency such as Laurence Barrett's *Gambling with History* (1983), William E. Pemberton's *Exit with Honor* (1997), Edmund Morris's authorized biography *Dutch* (2000), Lou Cannon's *President Reagan: The Role of a Lifetime* (2008), Sean Wilenz's *The Age of Reagan: A History, 1974-2008* (2009), Steven F. Hayward's *The Age of Reagan: The Conservative Counterrevolution, 1980-1989* (2010), Chris Matthews's *Tip and the Gipper* (2013), Jacob Weisberg's *Ronald Reagan* (2016), and Michael R. Adamson's chapter, "Reagan and the Economy: Business and Labor, Deregulation and Regulation," in Andrew L. Johns's *A Companion to Ronald Reagan* (2014) which had an extended section on the PATCO strike. Outside of the PATCO events themselves, political science analyses of the presidency in general, as well as of public opinion, coalition building, and administrative management in the Reagan presidency added valuable context, especially pieces by Michael Nelson, James W. Ceaser, Richard Nathan, and Benjamin Ginsberg and Martin Shefter. In particular, Richard Neustadt's classic exposition on the ingredients of *Presidential Power* helped frame the moment. Historical context was added by Michael Beschloss in *Presidential Courage* (2007).

Of course, journalistic sources such as the *New York Times*, *Washington Post*, *National Review*, *The New Republic*, and Associated Press and United Press International wire services were consulted, including some stories contemporary with the events and some reflecting back from ten, twenty, thirty, or forty years later. Also consulted were research papers produced by scholars, think tanks, and government agencies, as well as remarks found in the Congressional Record. The online archive of the Roper Center on Public Opinion offered an excellent resource for polling data.

Not least, the analysis here also relied on papers found at the Reagan Library. Particularly helpful were papers from Martin Anderson, Craig Fuller, David Gergen, Fred Fielding, Robert Bonitati, and Drew Lewis.

It is my hope that these resources have been brought together to provide a coherent and concise account of an important decision in presidential history.

INDEX

Page numbers in italics refer to tables or figures. Those followed by n refer to notes, with note number.

ACLU, 85
AFL-CIO
   and election of 1984, 101
   and growth of unions, 15
   personnel involved in PATCO strike, 36–37
   on potential impact of PATCO firings, 91
   Reagan as member of, 124
   Solidarity Day (1981), 82
   views on PATCO strike, 81–83
Air Line Pilots Association (ALPA)
   Bonitati and, 29
   endorsement of Reagan in 1980, 8
   PATCO's radicalization and, 21–22, 37
   views on PATCO strike, 83–84
   See also O'Donnell, J. J.
airlines
   and FAA strike contingency plan, 47, 85
   impact of strike on, 83, 89–90
   and injunction against PATCO strike, 51
   views on PATCO strike, 85
   See also Air Transport Association
air safety disruptions from PATCO firings, 90
Air Traffic Control Association (ATCA), 16
air traffic controllers
   activism prior to PATCO, 16–17
   cost of training, 90
   as federal employees, 4
   government reports on working conditions, 21
   number returning after threat of dismissal, 55, 139n64
   number striking and not striking, 55, 139n64
   oath of office forbidding strikes, 4, 49, 50–51, 54, 57, 68, 124–125, 137
   public's opinion of, 68
   replacement of, 55–56, 128–129
   responsibilities of, 4
   time required for training, 129
   unions after PATCO, 89
   See also firing of air traffic controllers
Air Transport Association (ATA)
   damages owed to, for PATCO strike, 36, 74
   and FAA strike contingency plan, 85
   and injunction against PATCO strike, 51, 74
   views on PATCO strike, 85
air travel disruptions from PATCO firings, 89–90
   costs to US economy, 90
   impact on airlines, 89–90
   as less than feared, 88
ALPA. *See* Air Line Pilots Association
American Bar Association, and PATCO strike, 85–86
American Federation of Government Employees, 37, 58, 81, 82, 91
An American Life (Reagan), 56–57, 104
American Postal Workers Union. *See* postal workers union
Anderson, John, 7, 27, 28
Anderson, Martin
   background and career of, 29
   on Reagan's management style, 32
   and Reagan's response to PATCO strike, 53, 57
   role in Reagan administration, 27, 29

158 INDEX

Andreas, Dwayne, 110
ATA. *See* Air Transport Association
Aviation Safety Institution, 90

Bailey, F. Lee, 17, 18
Baker, Howard
   and ban on hiring of strikers, 61
   Bonitati and, 29
   and PATCO contract negotiations, 42
   and PATCO pay rise demands, 71
   on Reagan's decisive decision, 106
   role in PATCO strike, 35–36
Baker, James III, 30–31
Barone, Michael, 93–94, 112–113
Barrett, Laurence I., 52, 56
Benda, Peter M., 32
Biden administration "State of Our Unions" report (2022), 99
Biller, Moe, 91
Blaylock, Ken, 37, 58, 91
Bond, Langhorne, 22, 40, 44, 63
Bonitati, Robert, 29–30
Braniff Airlines, 89–90
Britain
   frustration with repeated strikes, 65–66, 92
   Thatcher's coal strike response, 108–109
   Thatcher's election, conditions leading to, 65–66
Buckley, William F., 79
Bush, George H. W., 30, 61, 86, *98*
Bush, George W., *98*

Calhoon, Jesse, 21–22, 44
Canadian Air Traffic Control Association (CATCA), 34, 84
Carter, Jimmy
   and decline of union influence, 99
   and election of 1980, 7, 8, 22–23, 35
   foreign policy failures, 9–10
   ineffectiveness of, 11
   and PATCO job actions, 74
   and stagflation, 8–9

CATCA. *See* Canadian Air Traffic Control Association
Ceaser, James W., 107, 114
Chamber of Commerce, US, 85
Choirboys
   as lunatic fringe, in Leyden's view, 63
   as militant group within PATCO, 20
   miscalculations about strike, 65
   opposition to PATCO labor agreement, 44
   and Poli's takeover of PATCO, 20–21, 33
   and strike vote, 45
Civil Service Reform Act of 1978, 50, 59
Clay, William Lacy, Sr., 21, 35–36, 40, 46
Clinton, Bill
   decline in union influence under, 97–98
   number of strikes during administration of, *98*
   rescinding of FAA ban on rehiring of fired PATCO controllers, 89, 97–98
Colson, Charles, 19
Communism
   Reagan's opposition to, 5, 6
   US weakness of 1970s and, 9
Congress
   investigation of Reagan's promises to PATCO, 43
   and lawsuit demanding rehiring of PATCO controllers, 75
   leading figures during PATCO strike, 35–36
   opinions on PATCO strike in, 70–74
   and PATCO contract negotiations, 44, 46
   PATCO's failure to secure allies in, 74
   PATCO supporters in, 40, 46
   ultimate control over PATCO settlement, 34
consequences of PATCO firings, 88–89, 113–114
   air safety and, 90
   establishment of Reagan as forceful leader, 103–108

PATCO's actions and, 114
Reagan's determination to enforce the law despite, 114–115
restored confidence in presidency as institution, 104, 108, 113
as wide-ranging, 113
See also air travel disruptions from PATCO firings; economic consequences of PATCO firings; effect of PATCO firings on; international impact of PATCO firings; political consequences of PATCO firings; unions
Conyers, John, 72–73
Coolidge, Calvin, 6, 15, 56, 77, 79
Corson Committee Report (1970), 21
courts. *See* judiciary
COVID pandemic, union power and, 93

Deaver, Michael
and ban on hiring of strikers, 61
and PATCO contract negotiations, 42
on Reagan's response to PATCO strike, 52–53
role in Reagan administration, 30–31
Democratic Party
inability to rescue PATCO, 100, 115
Reagan's blunting of union power and, 100
Department of Justice
opposition to rehiring of controllers, 74
and PATCO contract negotiations, 43
prosecution of PATCO leaders, 52, 59, 74–75
See also Smith, William French
Department of Transportation
and FAA employment for fired PATCO controllers, 89
Lewis as head of, 25, 40
and PATCO negotiations, 40–41
See also Lewis, Drew
Devine, Donald J.
background and career of, 28–29
and ban on rehiring of strikers, 61
on benefits of reducing unions' power, 95
as director of Office of Personnel Management, 28
and PATCO contract negotiations, 42–43, 58
on Reagan's decision to fire strikers, 52
views on PATCO strike, 28
Donovan, Raymond, 58–59
D'Souza, Dinesh, 48, 104

Eads, Gary, 33, 59
economic consequences of PATCO firings
airlines and, 83, 89–90
increased growth with decline in union power, 94–96, 113
inflation reduction, 95–96
Economic Policy Institute, 98
Economic Recovery Tax Act of 1981 (ERTA), 13–14, 71, 72
election of 1980
Democratic primaries, 35
PATCO letter outlining conditions for endorsing Reagan, 23, 27, 39, 43, 49, 136n18
PATCO's endorsement of Reagan, 5, 8, 22–23, 27, 39, 49, 112, 115
Reagan's campaign staff, 26, 29
Reagan's decisive victory, 7–8
Reagan's letter to PATCO endorsing general goals, 23, 54–55, 62–63, 123
Republican gains in Congress, 8
unions and, 8
election of 1984, 101
ERTA. *See* Economic Recovery Tax Act of 1981
Executive Order 10988, 11, 15, 16, 17, 19
Executive Order 11491, 19

FAA (Federal Aviation Agency/Administration)
air traffic controllers as employees of, 5

FAA (Federal Aviation Agency/
    Administration) (*cont.*)
  concessions to air traffic controllers
    before PATCO, 16–17
  concessions to PATCO demands,
    17–18, 19–20
  Helms as head of, 40
  and PATCO contract negotiations, 46
  and PATCO founding, 16
  and PATCO negotiations, 40–42
  planning for PATCO strike, 22, 25
  poor relations with air traffic
    controllers, 5, 18, 20, 21, 24
  See also Helms, J. Lynn
FAA contingency plan for PATCO
    strike
  attention to, before strike, 41, 43
  details of, 47
  Helms's responsibility for, 25
  implementation of, 47, 51, 58,
    116–117, 124
  long planning process for, 22
  PATCO's underestimation of, 115
  publication of, 22
  and public opinion on strike, 68
  Reagan's monitoring of, 52
  replacement of air traffic controllers,
    55–56, 128–129
  risks of, 48
familiarization flights (FAMs), 19, 20
Federal Aviation Agency/
    Administration. *See* FAA
federal employees, laws forbidding
    negotiations of pay or hours, 19,
    22, 41, 44
federal employees, laws forbidding
    strikes by, 4, 50
  as basis of decision to fire PATCO
    strikers, 49–50, 52–53
  lack of ambiguity in, 55
  lax enforcement in before PATCO
    strike, 23–24, 51, 64
  penalties for violations, 50
  Reagan on, 54, 124–125

federal hiring of fired strikers,
    restrictions placed on, 60
  Clinton's rescinding of FAA ban on,
    89, 97–98
  congressional opinion on, 73, 74
  foreign policy considerations in, 110
  lawsuit demanding rehiring, 75
  media views on, 77–78, 79–80
  pressure on Reagan to reverse, 60–62
  public opinion polls on, 69–70
  Reagan's loosening of, 61–62, 87, 116
  union leaders' views on, 77–78, 84
Federal Labor Relations Authority
  decertification of PATCO, 59–60, 75
  on PATCO contract negotiations, 54
  and violations of federal no-strike
    laws, 50
firing of air traffic controllers, 51
  appeals to Merit Systems Protection
    Board, 88–89
  financial impact on controllers, 88
  number eventually rehired, 88–89
  pressure on Reagan's to reverse, 60–62
  Reagan press conference on, 124–129
  as success for Reagan, 1
  See also consequences of PATCO
    firings; federal hiring of fired
    strikers, restrictions placed on;
    reactions to PATCO firings
Ford, Gerald, 7, 11, 26, 30
Fraser, Douglas
  lawsuit demanding rehiring of
    PATCO controllers, 75
  PATCO strike involvement, 37
  views on PATCO strike, 81, 91
Fuller, Craig
  and ban on hiring of strikers, 61
  and PATCO contract negotiations,
    41, 42
  role in Reagan administration, 29

Gergen, David, 30, 51, 52
Ghilarducci, Teresa, 108–109
Goldwater, Barry, 6, 30, 46

INDEX 161

Greene, Harold H., 36, 74
Greenspan, Alan, 95–96, 114

Harvey, Paul, 78–79
Hearst, William Randolph, Jr., 78
Helms, J. Lynn
   background and career, 26
   as FAA director, 25, 40
   and PATCO contract negotiations,
      40–41, 45, 55
   and Reagan's response to PATCO
      strike, 51, 52
   views on PATCO strike, 26
   work with ATA against strike, 85
   work with Canada during PATCO
      strike, 84
Hinckley, John, Jr., 14
Hoover, Herbert, 15

injunction against PATCO strikes
   (1970)
   courts' refusal to vacate, 74
   history of lax enforcement of, 51, 64
   issuing of, 18, 24, 51
   PATCO fines for violation of, 51, 74,
      88, 125–126
   as permanent, 4
interest groups' responses to PATCO
   strike, 85–86
International Federation of Air
   Traffic Controllers' Association
   (IFATCA), 84–85
international impact of PATCO firings
   recognized importance of, 114
   Soviet respect for Reagan, 109–111,
      113–114
   and Thatcher's coal strike response,
      108–109
Iran-Contra scandal, 32, 56
Iranian hostage crisis, and PATCO
   strike, 68
Iranian Revolution, 9–10
Islamic jihadists, US weakness of 1970s
   and, 9–10

Jackson, Maynard, 91
January 6th, 2021, Capital riot, 103
Johnson, Haynes, 79–80, 106, 109
Johnson, Lyndon B., 11, 18
Johnson Report (1982), 21
judiciary
   and decertification of PATCO, 75
   fines against PATCO, 51, 74, 88,
      125–126
   and prosecution of PATCO
      leadership, 74–75
   response to PATCO strike, 74–75
   role in PATCO strike, 36
   See also injunction against PATCO
      strikes (1970)

Kemp, Jack, 13, 27–28
Kennedy, Edward M. "Ted," 8, 35
Kennedy, John F., 11, 15, 35
Kerr, George, 21, 22
Keynesianism, failures of 1970s, 7, 8–9
Kheel, Theodore W., 96, 114
Khomeini, Ayatollah Ruhollah, 9–10
Kirkland, Lane
   background and career of, 36–37
   opposition to Reagan agenda, 37
   on PATCO picket line, 50
   proposed alternative solution to
      strike, 57–58
   views on PATCO strike, 81, 83

law. *See* federal employees, laws
   forbidding negotiations of pay or
   hours; federal employees, laws
   forbidding strikes by
Laxalt, Paul, 106
Leighton, Richard, 23, 27, 39, 43, 49,
   136n18
Lewis, Drew
   appearances to sway opinion on
      PATCO firings, 78
   background and career, 25–26
   and ban on hiring of strikers, 61, 73
   on decertification of PATCO, 59–60

Lewis, Drew (*cont.*)
   and firing of PATCO controllers, 104
   and PATCO contract negotiations, 40–47, 49, 55, 56, 63, 113, 115
   and press conference on PATCO firings, 125–129
   and Reagan's response to PATCO strike, 51, 52, 53, 55, 58, 59
   as Secretary of Transportation, 25, 40
   views on PATCO strike, 26
   work with Canada during PATCO strike, 84
Leyden, John F.
   ejection from PATCO presidency, 20–21, 33
   Miller and, 63
   O'Donnell and, 37, 83
   on PATCO Choirboys, 63
   and PATCO contract negotiations, 45
   as president of PATCO, 18, 19, 20
Loomis, Erik, 81–82

Maher, Jack
   and founding of PATCO, 16, 17
   and PATCO local 6881, 89
   and PATCO's militant turn, 20
Major League Baseball strike, 68–69
Maritime Engineers Beneficial Association (MEBA), 18, 19, 21–22, 23, 36, 44
Mathias, Charles McC., 35–36
Matthews, Chris, 73
McCartin, Joseph A., 10, 23, 26, 42, 91, 103, 114
McGovern, George, 7, 8, 19, 37, 102
Meany, George, 15, 36–37
MEBA. *See* Maritime Engineers Beneficial Association
media
   on Reagan's strong leadership, 106
   response to PATCO firings, 75
   view on rehiring of fired controllers, 77–78, 79–80
Meese, Edwin III
   and ban on hiring of strikers, 61
   and PATCO contract negotiations, 41, 42
   on Reagan's decisiveness, 104
   on Reagan's reasons for firing PATCO strikers, 49
   and Reagan's response to PATCO strike, 51
   role in Reagan administration, 29, 30–31
Meltzer, Bernard D., 23, 55, 60, 68, 75
Merit Systems Protection Board, 88–89
Meyer, Robert E., 33–34, 84–85
Miller, Joseph S., 44, 63
Mineta, Norman, 46
Mondale, Walter, 101
Moody, Kim, 98–99
Morgan, David, 78, 80
Morgan, Lewis, and Bockius (law firm), 40
Morris, Edmund, 111

Nader, Ralph, 75
NAGE. *See* National Association of Government Employees
National Air Traffic Controllers Association (NATCA), 89
National Association of Government Employees (NAGE), 16–17
National Industrial Recovery Act of 1933, 14–15
National Labor Relations Act of 1935 (Wagner Act), 14–15
National Labor Relations Board
   hard line of Reagan years, 147n23
   pro-union members appointed by Clinton and Obama, 97–98
   Reagan's anti-labor appointments to, 100
National Review, 6, 79
National Transportation Safety Board, 90
Neustadt, Richard, 11–12, 107, 108
Nixon, Richard M.
   Anderson and, 29

and decline of presidency as
    institution, 11
and election of 1968, 29
and election of 1972, 7, 19
Gergen and, 30
management style of, 32
PATCO and, 19
and postal workers' strike, 23–24, 42–43
Noonan, Peggy, 110, 113
Nordlund, Willis J., 83, 91, 114
Northrup, Herbert R., 39, 92, 114

Obama, Barack, 97–98, *98*
OBRA. *See* Omnibus Budget
    Reconciliation Act of 1981
O'Donnell, J. J.
    background and career of, 37
    Leyden and, 37, 83
    and PATCO strike, 37
    Poli's takeover of PATCO and, 21–22
    views on PATCO strike, 83–84
Office of Management and Budget
    and FAA employment for fired
        PATCO controllers, 89
    role in Reagan administration, 32
    Stockman as director of, 27
    views on PATCO demands, 40, 41–42
Office of Personnel Management
    Levine as director of, 28
    on rehiring of controllers, 74, 89
    role in Reagan administration, 32
    views on PATCO demands, 42
Omnibus Budget Reconciliation Act of
    1981 (OBRA), 13–14
O'Neill, Thomas P. "Tip"
    political career of, 35
    on Reagan's handling of PATCO
        strike, 73
    role in PATCO strike, 35
    and Soviet respect for Reagan, 110

PATCO
    AFL-CIO association, 18
    aggressiveness of, 4–5, 19, 41
    air traffic controller activism prior to, 16–17
    decertification of, 51, 59–60, 75, 88
    early job actions, 17–18
    endorsement of Reagan in 1980, 5, 8, 22–23, 27, 39, 49, 112, 115
    founding of, 17
    gains after 1970, 18–20
    government's accommodation of past
        illegal strikes, 20–21, 23–24, 51, 64, 112
    history of, 4
    job actions before strike of 1981, 4–5, 19–20
    lack of good answers to Reagan's
        criticisms, 115
    leadership of, 5, 18
    letter on conditions for endorsing
        Reagan, 23, 27, 39, 43, 49, 136n18
    militant turn prior to 1981 strike, 20–22, 33
    organization as union, 17
    Reagan's efforts to accommodate
        demands of, 62–63
    Reagan's letter endorsing general
        goals of, 23, 54–55, 62–63, 123
    refusal of alternative solutions to
        strike, 57–58, 81
    sickout of 1970, injunctions ending, 18
    unions replacing, 89
PATCO strike
    Canadian Air Traffic Control
        Association (CATCA) and, 34, 84
    demands, 22, 23, 39, 40–41, 47
    and destruction of PATCO, 33
    government's success in replacing
        controllers, 47
    level of support within union, 43
    PATCO leaders' confidence in
        success of, 39
    PATCO officials overseeing, 33–34
    PATCO's aggressive threats of, 41
    PATCO's militant turn prior to, 20–22
    PATCO's reasons for optimism in, 5, 23–24, 104

PATCO strike (cont.)
　Poli as leader of, 33
　Polish Solidarity strikes Poland as model for, 10
　and Reagan administration concerns about presidential power, 11–12
　Reagan's budget cuts as context for, 13–14
　Reagan's position on, as clearly expressed, 45–46, 113, 115
　removal from civil service system as goal of, 39
　repeated denial of plans for, 22, 41, 46
　scholarship on, 1
　union's miscalculations, 62–64, 66, 115
　vote for, 45
　See also Reagan's response to PATCO strike
PATCO strike negotiations, 40–47
　cost of PATCO's demands, 54, 124
　potential repercussions for other federal unions, 42–43, 48–49, 95
　rejection of government offer, 43–47, 137n25
Pemberton, William E., 107, 108
pilots, views on PATCO strike, 83–84
Pipes, Richard, 109–110
Platt, Thomas C., 36, 74
Plum, Bernard M., 100
Poli, Robert E.
　AFL-CIO meeting with, 82
　on ALPA's lack of support, 83–84
　background and career of, 33
　on ban on hiring of PATCO strikers, 62
　character of, 33
　congressional critics on, 71
　on factors in PATCO's strike failure, 68
　on heavy fines against PATCO, 74
　as leader of PATCO strike, 33
　miscalculations about strike, 63
　and O'Neill's advice on strike, 73
　and PATCO contract negotiations, 41–44
　and PATCO's militant turn, 20, 22

　preparations for strike, 39
　repeated denial of strike plans, 22, 41, 46
　takeover of PATCO presidency, 5, 20–21, 33
　on unions' lack of support for PATCO strike, 80
political consequences of PATCO firings, 100–103
　blunting of unions' power, 100, 103
　Reagan's limited government philosophy and, 102–103
　Reagan's political capital enabling future successes, 107–108, 110–111, 113
　and Republican as working-class party, 102
　Republican wooing of unions and, 100–101
postal workers union
　contract negotiations, 48–49
　impact of PATCO firings on, 91–92
　strikes by, 42–43
presidency, as institution
　public's loss of faith in, before Reagan, 10–12, 105
　Reagan's force of character and, 104, 108, 113
Professional Air Traffic Controllers Organization. *See* PATCO
public opinion on PATCO firings, 65–70
　driving of other reactions, 86
　frustration with repeated strikes and, 65–66
　polls on, 66–70
　Reagan's responsiveness to, 116

railroad strike, Reagan's averting of, 100
reactions to PATCO firings
　in Congress, 70–74
　by interest groups, 85–86
　judiciary's response, 74–75
　by media, 75
　Reagan's astute political instincts and, 87

INDEX 165

Reagan's popularity and, 86
See also public opinion on PATCO firings; unions' response to PATCO strike and firings
Reagan, Ronald W.
  ability to highlight larger lessons within events, 112–113
  appeal to blue-collar voters, 101
  astute political instincts of, 87
  conditions leading to election of, 66
  as Democrat in early life, 5
  diary entries on PATCO strike, 49–50, 114–115
  exemption of PATCO from federal hiring freeze, 39
  general support of PATCO's public safety goals, 39–40
  as governor of California, 6–7, 31
  humor of, 14
  management style of, 31–32, 51–52, 56, 112–113
  and PATCO contract negotiations, 42, 46, 47
  and Poli, meetings with, 40
  political career, 6–7
  and railroad strike of 1982, 100
  Reykjavík summit, 62
  switch to Republican party, 6
  syndicated radio show, 7
  and unions, 5–7, 8, 10
  See also election of 1980
Reagan's presidency
  accomplishments and job approval ratings, 69
  early legislative successes, 12–14
  economic challenges, 8–9
  familiarity with values of Americans, 116
  forceful and effective leadership, 103–108
  foreign policy challenges, 9–10
  fortitude in rebound from assassination attempt, 106, 107
  on government as problem, not solution, 12
  important issues and decisions, 110–111
  inaugural speech, 12
  number of strikes during, *98*
  officials involved with PATCO strike, 25–31
  popularity after Hinkley's assassination attempt, 14
  and predecessors' perceived ineffectiveness, 10–12
  public's need for strong response to growing chaos, 105
  Reagan's persuasive power and, 14
  restoration of public's faith in presidency, 104, 108, 113
  spending and tax cuts, 12–14
  strategy for union engagement, 40
  "Troika" in chief of staff role, 30–31
Reagan's response to PATCO strike
  alternatives proposed by others, 57–58, 81
  broad lessons of, 115–117
  consistency with his past views, 53–54
  decertification of Union, 51, 59–60, 74, 88
  delegation of implementation, 55
  factors demanding strong response, 48–50
  fines against PATCO, 51, 74, 88, 125–126
  focus on duty to uphold the law, 114–115
  forty-eight-hour grace period, 51, 52, 54, 55, 125, 127
  illegality of strike and, 49–50, 52–53
  number of controllers returning after threat of dismissal, 55, 139n64
  options for, 47–48
  and power of moral arguments, 115–116
  press conference announcing, 53, 54, 124–129
  prosecution of strike leaders, 51, 52, 59, 74–75, 110, 125, 128–129
  Reagan's account of, 56–57, 59
  as Reagan's decision, 51–52
  risks of, 48, 116–117

Reagan's response to PATCO strike (*cont.*)
  strategic consistency and tactical flexibility in, 116
  supportive political context and, 116
  See also federal hiring of fired strikers, restrictions placed on; firing of air traffic controllers
replacement workers, Reagan's legitimization of, 93–94, 113
Republican Party
  efforts to win union support, 40, 100–101
  Reagan's switch to, 6
  rise in 1970s, 7
Rock, Mike, 16, 17, 20, 34
Roosevelt, Franklin D., 5, 7, 15, 16
Rose Report (1978), 21
Rumsfeld, Donald, 106

scholarship
  on PATCO strike, 1
  on Reagan's leadership, 106–107
Shostak, Arthur B., 68, 82, 84
Shultz, George, 110, 114
Skocik, David, 68, 82, 84
Smith, William French
  and ABA reaction to PATCO strike, 86
  as attorney general, 27
  background and career of, 27
  and press conference on PATCO firings, 125–129
  on Reagan's management style, 112
  and Reagan's response to PATCO strike, 51, 52
Solidarity strikes in Poland, as PATCO model, 10
Soviet Union
  aggression, and US failures of 1970s, 7
  respect for Reagan after PATCO firings, 109–111
"The State of Our Unions" report (2022), 99

Stockman, David, 27–28, 40, 42
Sunstein, Cass R., 23, 55, 60, 68, 75
Supreme Court, on federal no-strike laws, 50

Teamsters
  and AFL-CIO, 37
  and ban on hiring of PATCO strikers, 62
  endorsement of Reagan, 8, 23, 101
Teixeira, Ruy, 102
Thatcher, Margaret
  coal strike response, 108–109
  conditions leading to election of, 65–66
Trump, Donald J., *98*

unions
  decline, causes of, 99
  decline in number of strikes (1981–2020), 97–98, *98*
  declining influence since 1970s, 93–94, *95, 97,* 97–100, *98*
  era of concessions after 1979, 99
  history of progress made by, 14–15
  increased economic flexibility and growth with decline of, 94–96
  involvement in PATCO strike, 36–37
  lawsuit demanding rehiring of PATCO controllers, 75
  pattern bargaining and, 98–99
  political power, Reagan's blunting of, 100, 113
  Reagan and, 5–7, 8, 10
  Republican efforts to win support of, 40, 100–101
unions, effect of PATCO firings on, 90–101
  blunting of union's power, 100, 113
  drop in membership, 91
  increased economic growth with union decline, 94–95
  increased resistance to public sector unions, 92

increased union caution, 91–92, 96
legitimization of replacement
  workers, 93–94, 113
private sector impact, 93–100, *95*, *97*, *98*
public sector union membership and,
  92–93, *93*
restoration of union-government
  balance, 92–93
union decline since 1970s and, 93–94,
  95, 96–100, *97*, *98*
US avoidance of European-style
  labor chaos, 92
unions, public sector
effect of PATCO firings on, 92–93, *93*
and governments, power balance
  between, 92–93, *93*
history of progress made by, 15–16, 19
members as percentage of public
  employees (1949–2022), 92–93, *93*
prohibition on negotiations over pay, 19
prohibition on right to strike, 15, 16,
  18, 23–24
Reagan's views on strikes by, 113, 124
See also federal employees
unions' response to PATCO strike and
  firings, 80–85
activists' vs. rank-and-file views on, 84
AFL-CIO views, 81–83

Air Line Pilots Association views on,
  83–84
lukewarm support, 82, 86
reasons for lack of support, 80–81
support from unions abroad, 84–85
United Auto Workers
and AFL-CIO, 37
concessions to Chrysler (1979), 99
and PATCO strike, 37, 81
See also Fraser, Douglas
United Brotherhood of Carpenters,
  Reagan speech to, 59, 102
United Federation of Postal Clerks v.
  Blount (1971), 50
United States Air Traffic Controllers
  Organization (USATCO), 89

Volcker, Paul, 96, 114

Walker, Scott, 92
Wallaert, Steven L., 110
Wallison, Peter J., 52, 54, 95, 105, 113
Wilson, Woodrow, 15
Winpisinger, William, 37, 82
Wirthlin, Richard, 30, 67, 69–70

Young, Coleman, 73

www.ingramcontent.com/pod-product-compliance
Lightning Source LLC
Chambersburg PA
CBHW021157160426
43194CB00007B/776